Ms Blaelock's Book of Holistic Personal Finance

Also by Alexandria Blaelock

MS BLAELOCK'S BOOKS
Stress Free Dinner Parties
Signature Wardrobe Planning
Holistic Personal Finance
Minimally Viable Housekeeping

SHORT STORIES
Alma's Grace
Balancing the Book
Fate in Your Hands
Kiss of Death
Lady of the Looking Glass
Life in the Security Directorate
Long Weekend in the Snow
Love in the Security Directorate
Needy Bitch
Payton's Run
Phoenix Child
Shining Star
Ship in a Bottle
Simone Says Hands in the Air
The Guardian's Vigil
The Life and Death of Carmelita Basingstoke

Ms Blaelock's Book of Holistic Personal Finance

Alexandria Blaelock

BlueMere Books
MELBOURNE, AUSTRALIA

This book expresses a philosophy of personal finance and makes suggestions about the different types of financial decisions you may make concerning your life and death. The author is not an accountant, lawyer, or psychologist; this book is not intended to provide definitive advice, and any plans you make as a result of reading this book should be reviewed by competent certified or licensed professionals.

Copyright © Alexandria Blaelock, 2017, 2020.

Originally published as Holistic Personal Finance: How to pay for the life you want.

All rights reserved. No part of this publication may be reproduced, distributed or transmitted in any form or by any means, including photo-copying, recording, or other electronic or mechanical methods, without the prior written permission of the publisher, except in the case of brief quotations embodied in critical reviews and certain other non-commercial uses permitted by copyright law.

For permission requests, contact enquiries@bluemerebooks.com.

Ordering Information:
Discounts are available on quantity purchases. For details, contact orders@bluemerebooks.com.

Ms Blaelock's Book of Holistic Personal Finance/Alexandria Blaelock.

hardback ISBN: 978-1-925749-03-8
paperback ISBN: 978-1-925749-04-5
digital ISBN: 978-1-925749-05-2

Book Layout © 2015 BookDesignTemplates.com
Cover Image © RetroClipArt/Shutterstock.com

BlueMere Books
www.bluemerebooks.com

*In memory of my mother,
who spent only the coppers on herself.*

Wealth is the ability to fully experience life.

—HENRY DAVID THOREAU

Contents

Introduction	10
PART ONE: The Wealth Management Cycle	19
Vision, Mission, and Virtues	21
Goals	29
Spending Plan	39
Monitor and Control	57
Annual Review	73
Record Keeping	79
PART TWO: Managing Money	87
Spending Money	89
Saving Money	103
Sharing Your Bounty	121
PART THREE: Living with Money	127
Understanding Your Past	129
Borrowing Money	139
Managing Risk	149
Handling Your Health	173
Owning a Business	183
Buying Property	195
Marriage	203
Children	217
Divorce	233
Retirement	239
Estate Planning	251
Conclusion	261
Appendix A: Miss Baker	263
Appendix B: The Smiths	267
Appendix C: The Butchers	271
Appendix D: Sample House Deposit Spending Plan	275
Glossary	281
Bibliography	287
Index	291
Author's Note	296
About the Author	297

Introduction

WHEN IT COMES TO FINANCE, you are usually offered either/or options. You either seek to gather massive amounts of money (to the exclusion of all else), or you don't (and are therefore crazy).

Which is fair enough, since finance is all about the money.

But money is just bits of paper, plastic or moulded metal. Its value comes from the time you spend in places you don't want to be, doing things you don't want to do, that you swap for the things you need like food and shelter. And the things you want, like chocolate or the latest smartphone.

It's just the medium of labour exchange.

Once, the only labour you could sell was your brawn; your physical ability to lift and carry heavy objects, but in modern times it's more likely that you'll sell your brain power. The business of selling your brain is time consuming and often leaves you buying someone else's brawn for the tasks you no longer have the time to do yourself.

But wealth, on the other hand, is more than money. It's an abundance of something (e.g., a wealth of experience). In fact, in the Middle Ages, wealth meant happiness (from the root word weal, meaning well-being).

These days, you're more likely to feel the lack of time or health (physical or mental) than money. So, when it comes to a long, full, and happy life, you need to manage these other aspects of wealth too not just the money.

The relationship between time, money, and health can be demonstrated in a triangle (see Figure 1: Labour Exchange).

At almost any point of your life, your ability to get stuff done is limited by the time, money, or state of physical and health available to you.

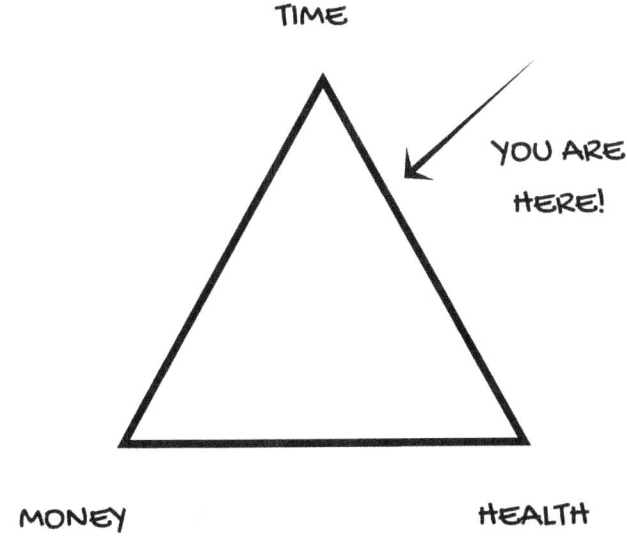

Figure 1: Labour Exchange

You can see that the arrow marks a point on the Time/Health axis. If your employer cuts your hours, but you want the same income, you have to choose whether to find additional hours elsewhere.

Working longer hours comes at a cost to your health, so you have to decide how much health you are willing to sacrifice for that income.

On the other hand, preserving your heath gives you less money but more time for activities that make you happy.

Maintaining your free time, leads to less income but potentially better health.

That's not to say it's an either/or proposition.

In reality, you move your arrows across all three axes according to the way your life unfolds.

For example, you decide to save money by cleaning your second-floor windows yourself, but you risk falling and injuring yourself.

Or you spend too much money on new clothes no one will see because you only wear them to watch television.

As a philosopher, I see the fundamental goal of life as increasing happiness and decreasing unhappiness. I don't mean happiness in the sense of a good mood, but the feeling of wellbeing that comes from enjoying a life you think is *worth* living.

Ancient Philosophers called this "flourishing"; an awareness of growing and developing, reaching to become something more than you were before. It might be "serving your country", "making glorious art" or something else. And the resulting feeling may be satisfaction, pleasure or similar.

It's not the money that makes you happy, but if you've the time and health to enjoy it, having some in the bank means you don't have to worry.

You have the opportunity to choose a fuller and happier life by focusing on what's important to you; the activities you pursue and the people you share them with.

Like your five morning minutes standing on the rug, you bought on honeymoon, drinking coffee from the mug you made at pottery class watching your kids play in the garden you planted out yourself.

Maybe your cat is purring in the sunshine on a window sill nearby, and you can hear your partner singing in the shower.

Your knowledge of what's important to you guides your spending from big events like getting married or booking a trip to the small purchases like magazines and chocolate bars.

You may have heard the expression "a means to an end" or perhaps a debate about whether "the end justified the means".

The end is the result you want, and the means the way you get there.

So, if you want to visit the Eiffel Tower, the tower is your end, and your means will probably be a combination of walking, driving and flying.

The means/ends debate comes from the moral philosophy of Immanuel Kant (1724 - 1804). He argued that people are valuable because they are people (an end in themselves), not tools (the means).

When you *choose* to spend money, you spend it on goods and services that increase your happiness. Which is a roundabout way of explaining that while many people think money is the end (happiness), it's actually the means to happiness.

Let's think about your Paris trip one more time.

You have to plan how you are going to get there. If you're flying, you have to examine your options based on what's important to you; flight duration, arrival time, legroom and so on.

You could call these your values; they guide your choices (means) towards your goal (end).

Which brings up another issue. The word "value" has become an expression of *both* means and end. It's a bit confusing, so let's take your home as an example.

The house you own is valuable; it increases your net worth, you can borrow against it, and you can put more money into it to increase its value (means).

But you don't buy a house just to store value; you want a secure and stable home to bring up your children, a comfortable place to enjoy your leisure time or its proximity to restaurants and nightlife (ends).

You don't value the house for itself, you "value" it as a home, for the lifestyle it provides.

It's a means to your end.

You can see we need another word to describe our values.

Fortunately for us, the Ancient Philosophers are once more on hand to help out with the concept of "Virtue".

While Virtue has grown a veneer of morality (good/bad or right/wrong), its original meaning was to develop excellence of character.

Our Ancient Philosophers believed developing excellence in beauty was just as virtuous as developing excellence in building houses.

It was the *effort* of devoting your lifetime to becoming something more that was important.

Some people, and particularly businesses, use values to guide their goals and work. That seems reasonable, but so often the values are nebulous concepts like "respect", "integrity", "teamwork" and "accountability".

These concepts often come with definitions that limit their applicability, and that's reasonable too, because value is a fixed point.

Any Realtor can give you a "value" for your house, but you won't know what it's worth until you sell it.

Nor will you know what "respect" really means until you're in a position to challenge that business, for example, trying to get a refund for your Paris plane tickets.

Ancient Virtues, on the other hand, are works in progress.

You get to define both your means and ends knowing they're movable and each is a step towards something bigger.

Coming back to your money, you need to develop virtues to guide your choices (means) across your lifetime.

Before you put this book down and walk away, think about how you got here, and you'll see that you're already doing this, though not consciously.

If you believe education is important, you've got some qualifications. Or, if you think life experience is important, you've probably travelled and done interesting things in other cities or countries. If your family is important, you've made choices about where to live and what work to do.

This book just guides you to think more deeply about your choices.

Still with me?

I'm assuming spending money is not bringing you happiness. It may be you're spending too much, or not thinking about what's important while you are spending it.

I'm sure you can give me reasons (excuses), but if you have a money problem, chances are it comes from spending more than you get.

And this is because you think about money as if it's separate from you. But it's as much a part of you as the brain that chooses (or not) how to spend it, and the hand that passes it over - it's the life you exchanged for it.

Most people offering financial advice tell you to *either* earn more *or* spend less. If you just stop buying takeout coffee every day, you'll save hundreds of dollars by the end of the year!

All very well, but there are a thousand things I'd rather give up first. If you were to tell me to stop buying coffee, I'd ignore you, and you would see me at the Café Parisien ordering caffè latte as the Titanic sank beneath me.

Of course, I'd only have access to the First-Class café because everyone else would be abandoning ship.

The Cost of Living is a calculation each jurisdiction makes about how much it costs to maintain a given standard of living. If you examine the list of goods your government uses for its price surveys, you'll find it includes some products you use but not others.

Your cost of living isn't the rational, objective thing your government collates, but a subjective interpretation of your thoughts and feelings about what you need for a happy life.

Your necessity is someone else's luxury, both of you choosing the standard of living that best meets your needs for food, pleasant surroundings, and aspirations.

Wouldn't it be nicer to pick a priority area to indulge in, while reducing your spend in other areas to compensate? If you enjoy take out coffee, buy and enjoy it guilt-free, but don't (for example) buy another electronic tablet as well.

Your priorities change as your life changes. At some point the latest fashions will be your most important thing, at another paying off your student debt, saving for a house deposit, or saving towards your retirement.

And this is another key point; you need to plan to make these things happen.

By the time you stop paid work, you'll need enough savings to generate an income that meets your cost of living.

Plus, you'll need to know how to fill the 168 weekly hours you won't be working or commuting.

That could be retirement at 65, but you might be financially independent sooner - it's just a matter of focus and scale.

It's going to take the rest of your life to develop the skills and habits you'll need for a comfortable and secure retirement.

Managing your investments and living within the income they provide. Opening your credit card statements, balancing your cheque account, and maintaining a balanced stock portfolio. Sharing with those less fortunate, and enjoying a show or nice restaurant as well.

You will create the life you want - you can have it all, but not at the same time.

Managing wealth over your lifetime is more about handling your fear of not having enough than it is about the money.

It's controlling your expectations and protecting your wealth so you can live comfortably for the rest of your life.

Managing your money ensures you will always have enough regardless of stock market crashes, inheritances, or job losses.

When you manage your time, you can spend it on the activities that make you happy.

And when you manage your health, you can enjoy your time and money to its fullest extent.

Notes

I've invented some families, to guide us through the wealth management cycle. You can check the appendices any time you want to refresh your memory.

> **The Baker Family**
> Emily Baker is a single woman in her mid-twenties. She lives at home with her parents but pays them board. She continues to perform her childhood chores, does her own laundry, and eats the meals her mother prepares. She has a college degree and an entry-level job in a big company.
>
> **The Smith Family**
> Bob and Amanda Smith are married, have two children (Daniel 8, Lisa 6), and a dog named Toby. They live in a mortgaged house in the suburbs. Bob commutes to the city, and Amanda takes care of the

house and children. Now that both children are at school, she volunteers at their school.

The Butcher Family
Ash and Jo are an older couple who've been in a committed relationship for 25 years. They live together in an inner-city apartment with their cats Tiger and Shadow. They both work long hours in upper-management jobs, so they eat out most of the time.

By the way, I'm using the term "partner" to denote husbands, wives, de facto and same-sex spouses. I also use legal and accounting terminology (explained in the glossary).

My one exception is that Accountants use the term "account" for different spending categories. To avoid confusion, I'm using the term "department". I also think it neatly captures the specialisation of activities while calling to mind the stores you could be spending your money in.

PART ONE: The Wealth Management Cycle

WEALTH DOESN'T GROW ON ITS OWN. You need to develop a growth focus and a systematic wealth management strategy to support your efforts. This part uses a business approach to explain how.

CHAPTER 1

Vision, Mission, and Virtues

PEOPLE WHO OWN BUSINESSES ARE often very focused on growing a business that generates enough income to cover its costs, and a bit more to live on.

This often involves developing:

- A vision statement describing its goal.
- A mission statement explaining how they're going to achieve the goal.
- Values explaining what drives them to achieve their mission.

Theoretically, these statements describe the company's core philosophy; its what, how and why. They underpin every decision made at every level.

Vision Statement

Your vision statement is an expression of what your ideal universe looks like, and your place in it. You could set it as an imaginary future, but if you want to make it inspiring and actionable, it's more useful to give it a long-term time frame of five to ten years.

For example, if you are in a "minority group" you may look for a world where all people receive equal consideration, but for your five-year time frame limit it to equal consideration under the law.

Or if you hope for a world without war, hunger, or corruption, you may restrict it to your community or state.

Visions don't have to be BIG, but they need to be big enough and inspiring enough to form a firm foundation for you to work from and towards.

It doesn't have to be A vision either. It can be a combination of ideas, as long as you can make it an inspiring and memorable statement, like a 140-character tweetable comment.

Life being what it is, things change often. You may marry and draft a joint statement as well as your own. And later have children and want a family statement to join your personal and couple statements.

Maybe you'll discover you have a terminal disease and that'll change your ideas too.

Because of this, rather than set and forget the vision, we'll be including it in an Annual Review Cycle (see Chapter 5).

But for the moment, just consider what you want right now. Let's take a look at what our families might say:

The Baker Family

Emily hopes to meet a nice boy and get married, but first, she wants to get her own place. Not necessarily buy right now because she wants to pay off her student debt and travel as well, but a little place she doesn't have to share, and can come and go as she pleases.

Her vision statement could be

> "I live debt-free in an inexpensive, cosy apartment with red geraniums on my window sill. My lovely neighbours water my plants when I travel."

The Smiths

Bob and Amanda are concerned about the world their children are growing up in. The air and water are polluted, the climate is changing, and there are additives in the food. They worry about the quality of education and feel they're not living in the kind of village they want bringing up their children.

They feel a move to a more rural location might be best, somewhere with a large yard to play in, plenty of space to grow fruit, vegetables and chickens. Somewhere in a close-knit community with a good school.

The Smith vision could be

> "We're part of a close-knit rural community, growing healthy produce, and our children are receiving a good independent education."

The Butchers

As they approach their retirement, Ash and Jo don't feel they spend enough time together. They want to nurture their relationship and pursue an activity together, perhaps cooking, or taking a Spanish class so they can travel. Maybe walk the 500-mile (790 km) Camino de Santiago, though they acknowledge they'd need to build their fitness and stamina for that. They'd also like to have a more active role in the lives of their nieces and nephews.

Their vision statement might be

> "A long, happy and healthy life, enjoying indoor and outdoor activities together. Building an enormous memory bank to share with our family."

As you can see, these are different impressions of what people may hope for, reduced into a simple, memorable statement.

They aren't detailed enough to plan, but they are detailed enough to imagine, and this is the key component of keeping your vision alive:

- The softness of your couch on your skin as you drink coffee and listen to the silence of being alone in your own home.
- Hearing birdsong and the wind in the trees as you sit on your deck with your family watching the sunset.
- Feeling the sun on your back, the strength in your limbs and smelling wild thyme as you walk.

Mission Statement

Your mission statement turns your vision into a reality. It's a plan explaining what you're going to do, how you'll do it and why. It doesn't have to be particularly detailed, it's a hint at how you'll proceed.

If your vision statement was set in five years' time, your mission is your three-year milestone.

It's another short, positive statement bringing your vision into reality.

- "Promoting equal consideration under the law through community action, and policy advocacy."
- "Ending hunger in my local community by seeking food donations and cooking at the homeless shelter."
- "Help sick animals by getting good grades and becoming a veterinarian."
- "Love God and serve people."
- "Treasure my children."

Like your vision, you may want to come up with joint or family missions as well.

Baker

"Commit to an abundant future with a Spending Plan that pays off debt quickly and maximises long-term savings."

Smith

"Prioritise the children's long-term interests with a healthier and happier lifestyle in a cleaner nutritive environment."

Butcher

"Treasuring our relationship by enjoying time together; getting fit, hiking in the country, cooking and speaking Spanish."

Virtues Statement

With your vision (big picture) and mission (medium size picture) taken care of, it's time to zoom in closer and think about what's important to you.

As I said in the introduction, these are often called values, but I prefer the term Virtues (the development of excellence).

Essentially, your Virtues are your means of bringing your vision and mission (ends) alive. They're like your road map, or these days your Global Positioning System (GPS).

Once you plug in your destination, the GPS calculates your route and rules out all the options that don't take you where you want to go.

And if you lose focus and get lost, it gently suggests you "turn around where possible" so you can get back on track.

You can have as many Virtues as you want, but they'll be easier to develop and incorporate into your life if you keep them down to a reasonable number.

What's reasonable depends on you, but most life coaches and advisers recommend somewhere between three and seven.

Each Virtue is both a core belief and a decision-making criterion relevant to your life right now. And like the other statements, you'll want to personalise it for your situation and revise it annually.

For example, if one of your Virtues is Honesty, you are committing to telling the truth in all circumstances. This may be difficult, particularly if you don't like hurting people's feelings. But if you hope for a career in politics, being known for telling the truth could be an asset.

Courage might translate into a career in the military, a commitment to visiting a dentist twice a year, or simply getting the spiders out of the bath yourself.

Simplicity could mean decluttering, less complicated financial arrangements or following a weekly menu plan.

Virtues are also opportunities for personal development so you can choose attributes you want to grow into, like Calm, Joy or Openness. And of course, you can describe this in a way that's meaningful for you.

If you look back through the Family visions and missions, you can see that they share themes, and these are an indication of where their Virtues lie.

Baker

While Emily wants marriage and a family someday, the virtues her statements suggest are important to her in the short-term are Independence, Prosperity and Freedom.

If she was inclined, she might add Affection and Friendship, or just leave it at three virtues for the moment.

She could also go a little further and define what they look like for the next couple of years, for example, Independence could mean developing self-reliance, or Prosperity learning about wealth management.

Smith

Clearly, Bob and Amanda think Family is the most important, and following (or because of) this, Health, Education, and Community or perhaps Connection.

Butcher

Ash and Jo have recognised they're in danger of losing touch with each other, and want to make their relationship their top priority so their first Virtue may be Love, Relationship, or Romance. And as they want to work on it together, another could be Teamwork.

They're focusing on cooking and an activity that requires a high level of fitness so they could round it out with Health or Well-being.

Summary

Your Vision, Mission and Virtues provide a guidance system helping you establish and enjoy a life worth living.

- Your vision statement describes your ideal universe in a five to ten-year framework.
- Your mission statement explains what you're going to do in the next three years to get part of the way there.
- Your Virtues are your core beliefs, decision making criteria and opportunities for personal development.

CHAPTER 2

Goals

ONE OF THE KEY COMPONENTS of a happy life is setting and achieving goals. It makes you feel like you're getting somewhere, but the crucial thing is knowing where your particular somewhere is.

That's why I suggested starting with a long-term Vision of your future (five years) and a medium-term Mission (three years) leading the way. Now it's time to add the short-term with some Goals.

A goal, is something that you can achieve within the time you allow yourself. I'm focusing on annual goals because our lives to date have been counted out by years; birthdays, school years and annual workplace reviews.

And those big New Year celebrations.

You can follow the same principles to develop goals of any duration, whether that's a month or a decade. The difference is in how you achieve them.

Goal Setting Frameworks

There are several frameworks you can use to put together your goals, depending on what they are.

SMART Goals

The most common advice is that goals should be SMART:

> **Specific:** Or well defined. Not that you want to travel, but that you want to sail around the world.
>
> **Measurable:** You have an indicator of progress. Your trip is made of smaller tasks (e.g., getting your passport and visas, travel vaccinations, and arranging pet accommodation). You can tick each of these steps off as your departure date comes closer.
>
> **Achievable:** That you can do it. If you get seasick, sailing probably isn't going to work. You may be better

cruising on a monster ocean liner or taking a bus across Europe.

Realistic: Is within the scope of your available knowledge, time and resources. That you have access to a sailboat and can go for a significant period of time without a regular income.

Timely: That the amount of time required is not too much or too little; for example, that you are not trying to circumnavigate the world in a fortnight.

SMART goals can be quite difficult, especially if you hope to develop a new Virtue.

Let's say you've decided to cultivate the Virtue of Honesty; you may have to get creative.

S: Be honest with one person, or about one issue.

M: Note the number of times you were tempted to lie, and the number of times you told the truth.

A: Give yourself some learner leeway, and be honest maybe 75% of the time.

R: You do have the ability to tell the truth, you just have to want to.

T: This year.

It kind of works, doesn't it? But it may be better to use a different approach.

HARD Goals

Life can be pretty messy – it's generally held together by passion. This means life goals don't always fit into a neat objective framework. They may be better expressed as HARD goals.

Heartfelt: You have a strong emotional attachment to the outcome.

Animated: You can vividly imagine and connect to that outcome.

Required: They are absolutely necessary for success.

Difficult: You need to learn, develop new skills, and grow as a person.

So, looking again at Honesty;

H: You are *really* tired of being a lying douchebag.

A: You can visualise trust building and relationships deepening.

R: You can't live a happy life without interacting with other people.

D: It's like a leopard changing its spots.

"Better" Goals

Sometimes neither SMART nor HARD goals are right. Sometimes you just want to do better this year than you did last year. To speak Spanish more proficiently, read more books, or improve your focus.

These kinds of goals are the best for developing Virtues. They're also a little gentler when you fail - rather than calling yourself a dishonest loser, you can take comfort from being more honest than you were before.

Rather than getting depressed about your "failure" and giving up, you can take a break, consider what strategies may be more useful, and start afresh.

Longer Term Goals

Some annual goals will be part of a larger plan. For example, our student whose mission was to "Help sick animals by getting good grades and becoming a veterinarian" has automatically set an annual goal of passing their exams until they graduate as a vet licenced to practice. But for this year, they could set themselves a minimum grade of 85%.

Stretch Goals

Ordinarily, goals should be achievable, but some people like to set themselves "stretch" goals. These goals are so ambitious they are seemingly impossible.

This can be very de-motivating if you're not passionate about the outcome, but if you are, they can inspire you to extraordinary lengths to achieve them. For you to achieve this goal, your end must fully justify your means.

Our veterinary student, for example, might set a grade goal of 99.55%, which will require extreme dedication to achieve. They must learn to study more efficiently and effectively. They will probably irritate their instructors and fellow students with their constant questions. They will have to sacrifice leisure time for more hands-on practice and may lose friends.

Wealth Management Goals

You may be wondering what this has to do with wealth management, but this is setting the stage for merging your financial goals with your lifestyle goals.

Your life goals, guided by your vision, mission and virtues, give you the opportunity to choose where to cut spending to give yourself the best chance of achieving your goals.

For example, given the goal of sailing around the world, you might cut all your spending back to the bare minimum to maximise your savings so that you can travel for longer (which will also put you in the habit of spending less which will help you to preserve your funds for longer).

Or if you're developing Honesty, you might reduce your clothing spend so you can buy more apology gifts for the people you offend.

Only you can decide which sacrifices are worth their cost.

Living a happier life requires a delicate balance. You have to manage the cost of achieving your goals without sacrificing your mental, physical or spiritual requirements.

For example, if Family is one of your Virtues, and you are too tired or thinking too hard about work when you get home to enjoy your time with them, you need to consider whether your work supports your vision or needs to change.

You could buy in help to get more time with your family, or acknowledge that right now (but not forever) it's more important to work so that you can get more secure housing even if it does cost you time with your family.

But back to the goal setting.

Like virtues, you can have as many goals as you like, but the more goals you have, the harder it is to achieve them.

Seemingly Warren Buffet advises an elimination strategy. First, write down the top 25 things you want to do. Then decide your top five and ignore the bottom 20 until you've finished the top five.

Every moment you spend tinkering with the bottom 20 is a moment you're not working towards what you really want.

Because they're built on your vision for the future, you may find that setting a goal with one virtue has flow on effects.

Our Honest person probably also has the Virtue of Discipline. Each time they tell the truth, they not only strengthen the Virtue of Honesty, but reinforce the Virtue of Discipline through the same act of will.

Similarly, our veterinary student probably has the Virtue of Caring in addition to Education, so by pursuing opportunities to care for animals they develop both.

Let's take a look at what our families could do. For the sake of page numbers (and book price), I'll illustrate one goal each.

Baker

With her vision of independence, and mission of an Abundant future, Emily has done some research and discovered that apartment rentals range from $500 - $1,000 per month, with establishment costs about the same.

Before she signs a lease, she wants to practice paying rent so she (and her parents) can be assured it's affordable, so she'll be attempting to save the equivalent of rent each month. But she wants to move somewhere nice (and safe), and will stretch her monthly savings goal to $1,100.

At the end of the year, she'll have achieved the habit of living on less and saved her deposit and first month's rent. She'll also have $13,200 she can use for establishment costs, to buy homewares for her new home, take a trip, or pay down her student loans.

Her SMART goal becomes:

> "This year, I will bank $1,100 each month in a high-interest savings account."

Smith

With the vision of moving to a cleaner, close-knit community and the mission of prioritising the children's interests, the Smiths decide it's time to move.

While they want to do it immediately, they agree it will be for the long-term, so they must be sure it's the right place.

They decide to research what they need, and where their needs can be met.

Their HARD goal is:

"We will shortlist five potential communities by the end of the year."

Butcher

Ash and Jo want to focus on the Virtues of Love, Teamwork and Health by cooking a meal together at home once a week.

Their GET BETTER goal becomes:

"We will grow our relationship by preparing and eating healthy food together."

Goal Planning

Goal setting isn't the end of the story - you won't achieve your goals if you don't lay out a plan for reaching them. Most people who don't make plans forget and abandon their goals by the end of the month they make them.

The plan is similar to the recipe you use to make a meal. It's a list of ingredients and the steps you need to take (your means) bring about the result you want (your end).

Baker

Emily's is relatively straightforward; she can open a dedicated savings account and have part of her pay deposited into it. She could even make it an account that's harder to withdraw from, for example, one that doesn't have an ATM card, or where she has to wait 24 hours for the funds to be transferred to her everyday account.

Smith

The Smiths have accidentally set themselves an enormous goal. The best way to proceed is to break the bigger goal into smaller steps within a logical framework. They should agree some responsibilities and time frames and add them to their calendars to make sure that they progress their goal.

For example, start by deciding some respectful communication ground rules. Allowing a month to agree their "must have" and "nice to have" attributes, and another to identify preferred and no-go countries or states. After a year of investigating the relative merits and cost of living in each area, they can rank them and pick their preferred location.

Butcher

Ash and Jo's goal is both easy and hard at the same time. They need to find some local classes at times they can both make, and schedule these along with Date Night as priority weekly appointments. They will need a conscious, ongoing focus (e.g., packing up and leaving work "early") until it becomes an automatic response.

Goal Reviews

Even with a plan, it's really easy to get distracted by life and forget about your goals or veer off track. You need to check in now and again to see how you're proceeding with your goals. I've included this process in Chapter 4: Monitor and Control.

Summary

Goals are steps towards achieving your mission and bringing your ideal universe into being.
- They can be SMART, HARD, or Better.
- Setting lifestyle goals helps prioritise spending and manage wealth.
- Planning to achieve goals is like writing a recipe with ingredients and steps.

CHAPTER 3

Spending Plan

Yes, technically it's a budget, but as most people don't like the feeling of restriction that word implies, it makes sense to avoid it.

I call it a Spending Plan to denote a more active and forward-thinking approach to your spending.

What is a Spending Plan?

At its core, your Spending Plan is just a tool for bringing your vision into reality.

When driven by your goals, rather than your income, it helps you get what you want out of life (which is why you need to do the vision work first).

It isn't supposed to limit your spending, offering no room for manoeuvre. It gives you the opportunity to choose where to spend and where to cut back.

It doesn't matter how small your income is, or how big your goals are, you create your plan according to your circumstances so that at the year's end you've come a little closer to the ideal life that inspires you. Whether that's a good education, a thriving business or a beautiful home.

The plan is a goal-based estimate of the cost of running your life; a comparison of what you want with what's possible. Seeing it laid out in black and white helps you to not spend more money than you expect to receive.

It's a very personal thing because *your* needs, desires, and family are different to everyone else's.

Some people have jobs that require high-status clothes and memberships. Some live in cities with good access to shops and public transport while others are in the country with less. Those in arctic regions and need warm clothes and climate control, but those in more temperate zones may prefer swimming pools.

The best and most useful Spending Plan gives you what you need to live a happy life, but doesn't demand sheer bloody-mindedness to stick to.

Why You Need a Spending Plan

Continuing the business context, there are three main reasons you need a Spending Plan:
- To forecast your income and spending as an indication of the sustainability of the life you are living,
- To help you decide whether you can afford unplanned spending, and
- To measure your progress.

It's a way of making sure that your spending is aligned with your virtues and goals.

If you make provisions across the year rather than living paycheque by paycheque, your money is there when you need it for the essentials, whether they are:
- Regular ongoing costs like food and housing, or
- Seasonal variations, such as winter fuel and clothing.

You can borrow from other Spending Plan departments when you want to, but it can be difficult if you need that money before you pay it back.

Planning your spending also ensures you do it at the right time and in the right places. As well as money for your immediate needs, you have the opportunity to maximise the income earning potential of your longer-term provisions.

For example, saving your winter spending in a high-interest account over summer and using the associated debit card to pay them when the time comes.

Developing a Spending Plan

You've created a vision, set yourself a mission, and chosen some virtues to develop. Now it's time to draw up a Spending Plan that fits your life.

You could adopt a generic Spending Plan, but it won't fit your life. It'll be like keeping an elephant as a pet in a small five storey walk up apartment.

It will pinch in awkward places, trash your living room and leave crap everywhere.

1. Add Up Your Income

Add up all the income you're confident of receiving this year, like wages (unless you are expecting to stop work), allowances, rents, government benefits and other income.

Don't include gifts, bonuses, or dividends unless you know with absolute certainty that they will come in. And if you're not sure how much money will be coming in, work to your lowest expectation.

Divide your total by 12 to get your monthly average. If you prefer to work with your pay period, divide by 26 for fortnightly, or 52 for weekly.

I'll be talking about months, but if you've decided to work with your pay period, substitute that.

2. Choose Your Departments

Just as a business has specialist departments (e.g., sales and marketing, customer service, and financial), your life has departments that categorise your activity and spending.

Handily, they fall into five major categories (in order of importance):

1. **Food**: probably be the most important purchases you make. The less money you have, the more you have to spend on food.
2. **Housing**: whether you own or rent, your home is the foundation of your life and sets its tone and scale. If you find that you need to cut costs, housing is generally one of the easiest places to do it.
3. **Clothing**: knowing what to buy, and how much to spend is an issue that many of us struggle with, and some of us spend a lot more than we really ought to. It's the second most significant item of household spending; savings and excess here will have the most impact on other departments.
4. **Operating Costs**: in the business context, operating costs relate to the resources required to keep a business going. Leaving aside premises (housing), this includes utilities, heating, phones, computing, cleaning, furniture, equipment, insurances, taxes, vehicles, maintenance, administration and wages.

    For you, these are the unavoidable expenses of life. This department also includes transient expenses like newspapers, medical care and children's activities.

    Operating costs are generally not controlled well, if at all. Almost all unplanned and emergency spending comes from here. And as most people don't plan or provide for routine maintenance and replacement, these costs can be enormous.
5. **Happy Life**: everything else. This department takes over when your basic needs are met, and you don't have to worry about them anymore. It's where the funds to achieve your goals comes from. You can add or include smaller specialities: for example, rent practice, research fund, Spain trip.

6. **Incidentals**: the small unexpected expenses that have a way of mounting up when you're not watching them. Your ad hoc lunches, a quick drink after work, or a magazine to read on the train.

    This is not a department per se, so it doesn't have a funding allocation. It's like the mail room; it's a place where you put unexpected expenses while you figure out where they belong or if you need to monitor them.

    Often incidentals are more about inaccurate accounting than unplanned spending, so if you see them frequently, or the cost is starting to add up, you should recast your Spending Plan to include them.

    I'm not saying that you must stop buying this stuff, I'm saying that they aren't incidentals and that you should be making provision for them. Give yourself pocket money for free spending, but draw boundaries around what it covers.

Once you choose your departments, and your proportional allocations, you must work within them. Consistently allocate the same costs to the same places, and try to make sure you've the money to pay for the basics, with some left over for saving.

3. Work Out Where Your Money Goes

Most people underestimate their spending by as much as $1,500 a month because they forget about the expenses that don't come up *every* month. Goods like contact lenses, insurances, and vacations.

Nor do they account for seasonal variations in the cost of services like heating, utilities, or yard care.

Or remember that months with five weeks cost more than those with four (e.g., cleaning, yard service and children's pocket money).

Plus, gifts, clothes, and so on for birthdays, parties, and events like weddings and Christmas.

Or unpredictable expenses like taxis, clothing repairs, and emergency dental work that isn't covered by your insurance.

You need a solid figure to work from, so set aside a few hours and collect together all the papers that indicate where your money has been going, for as many whole years, as far back in time as you have papers for.

This includes bank statements, credit card bills, ATM and store receipts, and if you live in a country that returns them to you, your paid cheques. The longer the period of time you have records for, the more likely you are to create a complete and accurate spending record.

1. Start laying your papers out in piles for each department; add or change them as you get a better idea of your expenses.

    You can include large departments, and smaller specialities if they meet your needs better. For example, you might plan Food, or split it into:
    - Dining in and dining out, or
    - Supermarket, butcher, baker, groceries, or
    - Food and alcohol.

2. Try to think forward as well as backwards because your vision and goals work may change your spending patterns.

    For example, if you are quitting smoking, think about what you can do with that money instead. If you have this type of goal, consider making "Quitting" a department of its own so you can watch your savings grow.

3. When you have allocated everything to a department, add each one to get a total cost.

4. Prices usually go up and rarely down, this is called inflation. Its general effect is that a dollar buys a little less each year; something that cost $10 in 1970 costs about $82 now.

   This is why your grandparents will tell you they remember the days when they could buy a quart of milk for 10¢.

   While inflationary changes are not usually very dramatic between adjacent years (e.g., 1970 - 1971), you would be wise to increase the total cost of each department by 2 - 5% to compensate (or by your prevailing inflation rate).
5. Then divide by 12 months to get as average monthly cost.
6. Add the departmental costs together to get your total monthly average.

Some months will cost more and some less, but if you want to end the year without additional debt, your monthly income must at least cover your average monthly cost.

4. Can You Afford Your Life?

Chances are, you spend more than you earn, which leaves you with three sensible options:
- Earn more.
- Spend less.
- Both (depending on how your situation looks).

If you're not sensible, you can carry on as you are, in the full and certain knowledge that your debt is increasing and you *are* headed for bankruptcy.

This is not the time for knee-jerk reactions or placing unreasonable expectations on yourself.

This is the time for you to consider your vision work and make some decisions about what you can realistically do to improve your circumstances.

Can you change jobs? Is it feasible to take a second job?

Your immediate answer might well be no.

You may be working so hard on two or three casual jobs to make ends meet that you don't have time to look for steadier work; assuming there is any out there to find.

And you might spend half the night working on a little business "on the side" as well.

In that case, it's more practical to consider spending a little less here and there to bring your overall costs down.

It's also a good time to choose which department is your priority so you can decide where else to reduce.

This is not an excuse to spend more in this area, it's just acknowledging that it's important to you and your circumstances are very dire if you have to cut costs here.

5. Define Your Costs

You have many types of costs; some more flexible than others.

Fixed and Variable Costs

Some costs, such as rent, mortgage and taxes, are fixed; and unchanging (for a period of time at least). They're predictable, and you have little control over them.

But most of your costs are variable; at any time, they can go up or down, though it has to be said that down is less likely, and many suppliers increase their rates at least annually.

You can deal with these in different ways:
- Build delays into your plan, for example, getting your hair done every eight weeks instead of six, or using the car wash every other week.

- Changing habits, like turning off lights and closing doors leaving rooms or naming some types of food "treat foods" that you eat less frequently.
- Schedule seasonal purchases like heating fuel for mid-summer when it is cheaper, and major purchases like new appliances for the sales.

You can find out how to reduce costs on almost every purchase you might conceivably make with an internet search.

Necessary and Unnecessary Costs (Needs and Wants)
In life, you need some things, and others you don't.

In 1943, Abraham Maslow started thinking about what human need consisted of, and he proposed a hierarchy of six levels of need:

1. **Physiological:** the stuff you need to survive; food, clothing and shelter.
2. **Safety:** financial, physical, health.
3. **Love and Belonging:** friends and family.
4. **Esteem:** the need for respect.
5. **Self-actualisation:** personal development.
6. **Self-transcendence:** thinking beyond the self to the benefit of others.

If you want to live, you must satisfy the first level of need; our first three departments are at this level.

- You *need* to eat (necessary), and if it were a choice between rats and nothing, you would eat rat even though you *want* lobster.
- You *need* clothing for warmth, protection from the elements, and to avoid being locked up for public indecency. You may *want* designer clothes, but you will wear whatever you find in the dumpster if that's all you can get.

- You *need* shelter, whether that's a box under a bridge, your car on the street or a beach front apartment.

Once you get past Maslow's first level of need, you move onto operating costs, and spending starts to become less about survival. You can take wants as well as needs into account; you can choose services and suppliers according to the features they offer that are more relevant for you and your virtues.

The third and higher levels contribute to happiness. This is where wants start outweighing needs. These days you probably *need* a phone, but any phone will do. You can make phone calls just as well on an old hand set as you can on the latest smartphone, but you *want* the smartphone (or nothing).

Wanting can have a profound effect on your life.

When you want, say that smartphone, your present and future are in conflict. You wish you already had one, and imagine your future is better than your present *because* you have it.

The wonderful thing about wanting is that it stops when you buy the smartphone and start enjoying it.

But it's not the phone you want, it's that moment of contented freedom from wanting. Sadly, it doesn't last long, and soon you'll start wanting the next model.

Knowing this, you don't have to allow wanting to control you; with your vision and goals in mind, you can make better decisions that bring them to fruition.

6. Tailor Your Spending Plan

At this point, you've already more or less created your Spending Plan; you know how much you've been spending, and how much income you're expecting.

Now you choose which departments to cut costs in so your overall costs are the same, or ideally less than your income.

How much you spend on each of these will be different depending on your income, family, and vision work. Some of the Spending Plans I've examined have wide ranges:

- **Food** (9 - 62%): Take a look at what you've been spending on food and decide whether there's an opportunity for change.

    If you can keep it under 25% of income, that's great, but if your income is low, you may need to increase this to as much as two-thirds.

    It doesn't necessarily need to go down; if you are pursuing Health, it may need to go up as you buy fresh produce to cook yourself.

- **Housing** (12 - 35%): In 1915, 20% of your income was considered a reasonable provision for housing, and anything more than 25% was extravagant.

    It makes a good starting point, but you need to think about your goals when you work out how much you're willing to pay.

    If you are a double income family saving for a trip to Spain, 20% may be too much, but if you are the sole parent of seven, it's probably not enough.

    Regardless, make this amount as small as you possibly can without making too great a sacrifice.

    Remember, a little extra rent (or mortgage) a week adds up to a great deal more over the space of the year.

- **Clothing** (12 - 20%): In 1915, when most men's clothing was ready-to-wear, and women's made-to-measure, 15% was considered a reasonable proportion of income to spend on clothing.

    Lucky Emily gets this all to herself! But as this is her first job, she'll need to think carefully about how she spends it.

The Smith family would proportionally split it between them (say Bob 35%, Amanda 23%, Daniel 22%, and Lisa 20%).

Ash and Jo would work out some sort of split, perhaps according to job seniority.

If you're wondering whether this figure still stands up to scrutiny, I did some analysis for my book *Build Your Signature Wardrobe*, and found that for me at least, it was a reasonable starting point.

You will, of course, need to consider this in light of your own vision, mission, virtues and income.

- **Operating Costs** (5 - 29%): While the early twentieth-century estimate was 15% of income, our modern lives include a lot more stuff in this department.

    Luckily, it also provides the most scope for cutting costs. Similar to the Clothing department, this will probably require Discipline, because much in this department is driven by external appearances, for example having the "right" car and furnishings.

    You'll probably also need Determination because there will be a lot of cost comparison and this can seem like too much work for too little reward.

    Happy Life (0 - 25%): If your income is small, this allocation must be too, and carefully managed to get the best value. You will feel happier if you can at least make a tiny provision for little luxuries, if not savings for your future financial independence, and sharing your bounty with those less fortunate than you.

    Enjoying life doesn't have to cost a great deal, and it doesn't have to be dull either. There are a lot of free and heavily discounted leisure activities you can pursue (e.g., concerts, museums or art galleries), all you have to do is find them.

While you shouldn't save money at the expense of your present comfort, you shouldn't make your present too comfortable at the cost of your future either.

The department names we've been working with are functional descriptions of the money's purpose. You might prefer to give them more exciting or meaningful names that inspire you to make wiser choices. Living, Castle, Costuming, Functioning and Higher Life anyone?

The important thing is to make your needs fit your income. Finding out you can't afford something after you've done it is not a comfortable or sustainable way to live because fixed incomes don't stretch.

But at the same time, don't assume that your income is only fit for particular kinds of expenses.

Bear in mind that costs in some departments will create savings in others (e.g., a house with a garden could save money on childcare, and when you grow your own produce, on food).

And the little bit of money saved each pay will result in a larger lump sum in the long term.

If Your Income is Unreliable

Most financial advice still comes from the assumption that your reassuringly dependable pay can be cut into small pieces. It can be hard to see how a spending plan might work if that's not your life.

If your income is not regular, predictable, or reliable, you'll need to rely on savings to carry you through the months you don't bring in enough to cover your costs.

This is a frightening position to be in, so make conservative estimates and base your Spending Plan on 75 - 90% of your projected income, according to how pessimistic you feel.

There are three additional techniques you can use to bring an element of reliability to your finances.

1. **Determine Your Minimum Viable Income:** Define your necessary and unnecessary costs according to your virtues. The absolute minimum income you need to bring in is the cost of your necessities. You just have to work out how to get it.
2. **Apply Business Practices:** Businesses continually seek to cut costs and increase income; purchasing is planned and researched.

    They'll compare purchasing and operating costs, ensure all available tax breaks are applied, and choose the products that offer the most cost-effective life.

    Production is planned according to seasonal demand, component availability, and to eliminate waste as far as possible. Obsolete equipment sold off at the end of its useful life.
3. **Ruthlessly Cut Costs:** Reducing your spending has the same effect as increasing your income.

    The harder you cut, the more you have, though this approach is probably not sustainable for the long term.

    You'll need some longer-term creative thinking to make the most of your modest spending.

    For example, taking excellent care of your clothes to extend their usable life or buying seedlings and growing vegetables, so you don't have to buy them later.

When Things Are Very Dire

There is no doubt that life can be very tough, and much of this book will seem completely irrelevant.

You *are* living in a cardboard box, eating rats, and wearing Dumpster Couture.

It's terrifying, and your pride is hurt because being broke is more about feeling powerless than not having money.

At times like these, you need to predict your cashflow; plot the dates and amounts of income against the dates and amounts of your expenditure.

When you look, you may notice issues like your electricity bill being due the week before you get paid. Knowing this gives you choices:

- Minimise expenditure further to save up for the bill.
- Reduce your power use to reduce the bill.
- Call your supplier to arrange a late payment.
- Ask your bank for a short-term overdraft.
- Bury your head in the sand and pay the late fees.

There's no point fussing about how you got here; choose to believe that your situation is temporary and move forward doing whatever you need to do to change it.

If you can't, your only alternative is to abandon hope, allow yourself to drown in a sea of misery and die of cold and starvation on a street corner.

Given courage and a sense of humour, you won't starve.

Important things like friendship don't rely on money. Your friends will want to help because they don't want to see you suffer (and they fear that one day they will need your help).

But they can't help you if you won't let them.

From the bottom, every direction is up.

Things You Can't Afford to do

Unless you're so lacking in spirit that you're drowning in that sea of misery and just don't care anymore.

- **Let Yourself Go:** letting go affects not just your self-esteem, but your job prospects and your partner's self-esteem too.

  It's human nature to look for scapegoats and people who don't appear to take care of themselves make an easy target. Personal grooming doesn't take long, and needn't cost much.
- **Pinch pennies:** it's not the same as wise economy.

  It makes you seem troublesome and demanding and can cost more in the long run.

  For example, a lack of ongoing household maintenance will require significant repair and cost more than a collection of minor jobs. The contractors you eventually hire are unlikely to give your run-down house their best work.

  Similarly, maintaining your furniture, replacing worn out linen and broken crockery as you go can be cheaper than waiting for it all to deteriorate past use and replacing it lump sum.

  Penny-pinching also has an effect on the self-esteem of your partner and the warm affection of your friends, and could result in the absence of both.

Summary

Planning your spending helps you:
- Plan your expenditure to get the best value.
- Save for big purchases.
- Identify areas where you can cut back.

CHAPTER 4

Monitor and Control

YOUR SPENDING PLAN IS LITTLE use if you don't use it to guide your spending. To make the most of it, you need a system to record your spending so you can compare it to your plan, and this system is called bookkeeping.

Bookkeeping is a business process, but it's just records of exchange; purchasing goods in return for cash. The records are entered into "accounts" or "the books", and you use the information to analyse your costs and decide how to control them.

The same principles apply to big and small businesses, and they work just as well for individuals and families.

This section refers to "books", and is illustrated with pictures of account books, but you can use any sort of notebook, computer file or app to record the dates, details and amounts of items you produce, exchange, consume and save.

It doesn't matter what you use, as long as you use it, because any record is better than no record. The best "book" for you is the one you find so easy to use, that you do in fact use it.

However, taking notes by hand allows you to more fully understand data and related concepts, so it may be worth doing this the old-fashioned way. Paper books are also useful when you are reviewing spending with other people as you are all literally on the same page.

Plus, you can note explanations, reprioritisation, or updated resolutions on the page when you make them, and sign to indicate your agreement to abide by the decision.

Transaction Basics

All financial transactions take place between a debtor who owes money to a creditor.

Let's use your job as an example; you provide services to the company before they pay you. You are the creditor, and your employer is the debtor that owes you money.

Conversely, when you hire a yard service, they do the work before you pay them. You're the debtor and the service the creditor you owe.

Complicated as this sounds, it's important because your books include money coming in and going out; debits when you incur debts and credits when you pay them off.

Keeping Books

When you set up your Spending Plan, you pulled together all your papers to work out how much you were spending.

Now you're going to start recording it as you spend it. This lets you see what and how you're spending, and change your habits if you need to.

I'll get to that later - first, you have to start recording so there's something to see. The full set of business books are:

- **Journal:** a record of the daily movement of cash. This could be by function (e.g., purchases), or by person (e.g., sales representative #2).
- **Ledger:** a record of the same daily movement of cash listed by department.
- **Balance sheet:** a statement of current financial position. In the personal context, it's often called a Statement of Net Worth (see Chapter 5: Annual Review).

For personal finance purposes, I recommend a single combined journal-ledger. You'll record income (from wages, rents, dividends, and so on) and expenditure (goods, services, durable utilities and investments).

Generally, a set of books lasts for one accounting cycle; the fiscal year. Depending on whether you do tax returns or not, you could do the same, or open a new set each January. During the year, you record your spending, and reconcile and balance your books monthly (or pay period).

At the year's end, you use the information in the ledger to create a Statement of Net Worth (carrying the cash and credit into a new book). This gives you the power to consciously manage your spending, plus start and grow a savings fund.

"Books" follow a standard format with income on the left, spending on the right, and totals on the far right. Each month opens with cash and account balances brought forward from the previous month and closes with totals for the month.

As well as date and details, the simplest form of book (see Figure 2) will have a column on the left for income, and a column on the right for spending.

DATE	DETAILS	INCOME	EXPENSE
01-Jun	Cash in Hand	$4	
01-Jun	Grocer		$116
01-Jun	Mortgage		$866
02-Jun	Supermarket		$206
02-Jun	Savings		$122
02-Jun	Pharmacy		$37
03-Jun	Phone		$20
04-Jun	Cooking/Heating Gas		$239
06-Jun	Bookstore		$5
06-Jun	Vegetables		$20
07-Jun	Public Transport		$50
22-Jun	Coffee & Cake		$9
23-Jun	Men's Clothing		$169
23-Jun	Grocer		$31
24-Jun	Pharmacy		$75
25-Jun	Rewards	$50	
26-Jun	Women's Clothing		-$227
26-Jun	Clothing Alterations		$10
27-Jun	Health Insurance		$184
27-Jun	Photos		$5
29-Jun	Grocer		$67
29-Jun	Supermarket		$79
30-Jun	Salary	$3,435	
30-Jun	Butcher		$28
	Balance $225	$4,015	$3,789

Figure 2: Simple Account Book

If you spend more often or need to monitor daily spends (e.g., your vacation spending), you could include a details column for both income and spending (see Figure 3).

DATE	INCOME		EXPENDITURE		
	Souces of Income	Amount	Nature of Expenditure	Amount	Daily Total
01-Jun	Cash in hand	$4			
			Grocer	$116	
			Mortgage	$866	$982
02-Jun			Supermarket	$206	
			Savings	$122	
			Pharmacy	$37	$365
03-Jun			Phone	$20	$20
04-Jun			Cooking/Heating Gas	$239	$239
06-Jun			Books	$5	
			Vegetables	$20	$25
07-Jun			Public Transport	$50	$50
22-Jun			Coffee & Cake	$9	$9
23-Jun			Men's Clothing	$169	
			Grocer	$31	$200
24-Jun			Pharmacy	$75	$75
25-Jun	Rewards Redemption	$50	Women's Clothing	-$227	
26-Jun			Clothing Alterations	$10	-$217
			Health Insurance	$184	
27-Jun			Photos	$5	$189
28-Jun			Grocer	$67	
29-Jun			Supermarket	$79	$146
30-Jun	Salary	$3,435	Butcher	$28	$28
	Total	$4,015	Balance $225		$3,789

Figure 3: Daily Spend Account Book

The journal ledger shown in Figure 4 uses a two-page spread with the spending split into departments. You can subdivide these into the specialities you are monitoring. If you are using an Incidentals column, it sits at the end.

DATE	RECEIPTS		FOOD				HOUSING		
			S'market	Grocer	Butcher	Takeout	Mortgage	Maint	Garden
01-Jun	Cash in Hand	$4		$116			$866		
02-Jun			$206						
03-Jun									
04-Jun									
05-Jun									
06-Jun				$20					
07-Jun									
08-Jun									
09-Jun			$41					$52	$232
10-Jun									
11-Jun									
12-Jun	Expense Claim	$526				$65			
13-Jun									
14-Jun									
15-Jun									
16-Jun									
17-Jun									
18-Jun						$14			
19-Jun			$436						
20-Jun						$28			
21-Jun						$90			
22-Jun						$9			
23-Jun				$31					
24-Jun									
25-Jun	Rewards	$50							
26-Jun									
27-Jun									
28-Jun									
29-Jun	Grocer		$79	$67					
30-Jun	Salary	$3,435			$28				
MONTHLY TOTALS		$4,015	$762	$234	$28	$205	$866	$52	$232
GROUP TOTALS				$1,230				$1,150	
				7%				14%	

Figure 4: Two Page Journal Ledger with Expenditure by Departments

You can see that food spending is split into Supermarket, Grocer, Butcher and Takeout. The owner of this book is monitoring clothing purchases, as well as the cost of alterations.

If you follow June 4 across the pages, you can see spending in the Food, Housing and Happiness departments, to a total of $425. The monthly departmental spends are at the bottom of the page along with the percentage of budget spent.

Holistic Personal Finance

CLOTHING			OPERATIONS				HAPPINESS					INC.	DAILY
Mr	Mrs	Alter	Phone	Post	Trans	Utilities	Dogs	Gifts	Ent.	Medical	Savings	Lost	TOTAL
													$982
										$37	$122		$365
				$20									$20
						$239							$239
													$0
									$5				$25
					$50								$50
													$0
											$100		$425
													$0
													$0
						$43							$108
													$0
													$0
	$44							$50					$94
					$18							$23	$41
						$200							$200
													$14
					$28						$100		$564
					$15								$43
							$95				$4		$189
													$9
$169													$200
											$75		$75
													$0
	-$227	$10								$184			-$33
								$5					$5
													$0
													$146
													$28
$169	-$183	$10	$20	$18	$136	$439	$95	$55		$296	$326	$23	$3,789
		-$4				$613					$772		
		0%				10%					7%		

Keeping to the page per month format gives you a high-level overview. If you find that you want more detail, you may need to use a separate journal to record your daily transactions, transferring the bulk totals into the journal-ledger.

If you are juggling credit accounts, you might prefer to use a journal-ledger more like the one shown in Figure 5, the left side uses a cash book format, and the right side the ledger.

DATE	INCOME		Expenditure	CASH		VISA	
	Income	Amount		Sums	Daily Total	Dr	Cr
01-Jun	Cash in hand	$4	Grocer				$116
			Mortgage	$1,666	$866		
02-Jun			Supermarket				$206
			Savings	$122			
			Pharmacy	$37	$122		
03-Jun			Phone				$20
04-Jun			Cooking/Heating Gas				$239
06-Jun			Books				$5
			Vegetables	$20	$20		
07-Jun			Public Transport				$50
09-Jun			Hardware				$52
			Plants				$132
			Supermarket				$41
			Savings	$100			
			Gardener	$100	$200		
12-Jun	Expense Claim	$526	Car Fuel				$43
			Takeout	$65			
15-Jun			Women's Clothing				$44
			Donation	$50	$50		
16-Jun			Postage	$18			
			Lost	$23	$41		
17-Jun			Electricity				$200
18-Jun			Takeout	$8			
			Coffee & Cake	$6	$14		
19-Jun			Supermarket				$436
			Postage	$28			
			Savings	$100	$564		
20-Jun			Takeout	$28			
			Parking	$15	$43		
21-Jun			Veterinarian				$95
			Restaurant				$90
			Savings	$4	$4		
22-Jun			Coffee & Cake	$9			
23-Jun			Men's Clothing				$169
			Grocer				$31
24-Jun			Pharmacy				$75
25-Jun	Rewards Redemption	$50				$50	
26-Jun			Women's Clothing			$227	
			Clothing Alterations	$10			
			Health Insurance		$10		$184
27-Jun			Photos	$5	$5		
28-Jun			Grocer				$67
29-Jun			Supermarket				$79
30-Jun	Salary	$3,435	Butcher		$709		$28
	Total	$4,015	Balance $225		$2,648	$277	$2,402

Figure 5: Two Page Combined Ledger Journal

The left side journal (cash book) includes the date, income, purchase detail and daily spend. The right side ledger lists spending by department and the total daily spend for both cash and credit.

Holistic Personal Finance

MASTERCARD Dr	MASTERCARD Cr	Food	House	Clothes	Ops.	Happy	Inc.	Daily Total
		$116						
			$866					$982
		$206						
						$122		
						$37		$365
					$20			$20
					$239			$239
						$5		
		$20						$25
					$50			$50
			$52					
			$132					
		$41						
						$100		
			$100					$425
					$43			
	$65	$65						$108
				$44				
						$50		$94
					$18			
							$23	$41
					$200			$200
		$8						
		$6						$14
		$436						
					$28			
						$100		$564
		$28						
					$15			$43
						$95		
		$90						
						$4		$189
		$9						$9
				$169				
		$31						$200
						$75		$75
				-$227				
				$10				
						$184		-$33
						$5		$5
		$67						$67
		$79						$79
		$28						$28
$0	$65	$1,230	$1,150	-$4	$613	$777	$23	$3,789

The ledger includes credit and debit columns for each credit account. Purchases are credits (because you owe them) and payments debits. Payments go in the journal (left) side as cash expenses and debits in the ledger (right).

If you don't work in the finance industry this does look backwards. You can do it the other way around if that's easier; just be consistent so you know what your position is.

If you always follow this pattern, you can quickly identify the balance owing during your reconciliation and pay it off.

These days you're unlikely to have accounts with individual suppliers, but you may find it useful to have a set of columns for each of your credit cards, particularly when you're paying them off (see Chapter 11: Borrowing Money).

Taken all together, this book shows:
- Your daily cash balance and financial situation.
- How much you owe to each of your creditors.
- Daily cash spends.
- Total cash/credit expenses.
- The current cost of each department.

Reconciling Your Books

Reconciliation is the process of "proving" the correctness of your books. It's also called "balancing" the books.

In business, it's a monthly activity, but you should match your Spending Plan frequency. There are two kinds of reconciliation you need to do.

Bank or Cash Reconciliation

1. Add each day's spend to find your total spend.
2. Add your current bank balance and cash on hand to get your current financial position.
3. Deduct your current position from the start balance.
4. The difference between your starting and current balances should equal your actual spend.

If the numbers don't match, you've either made a mistake in your calculations or forgotten to write a transaction down.

If you're monitoring expenses on credit, bear in mind that some purchases take longer to reach your account than others. You could add a "Lost" column to monitor this if you want.

Spending Plan Reconciliation

1. Add up all the spending columns to get the total spend for each department.
2. Compare this to your Spending Plan provisions (for the sake of convenience you might like to note this on the page as in Figure 3).

Ideally, your actual spend is the same as your planned.

It's useful to keep a copy of your full Spending Plan in the back of your account book for easy reference.

As the year progresses, you could note your actual monthly spend on it. This helps you monitor your overall annual spending, and results in a simple comparison of actual against planned at the end of the year.

Monitoring Your Spending

Reconciling your books is part of tracking your spending.

Monitoring is the process of observing and checking what you spend; you're looking for times when your actual spend is more or less than planned.

Perhaps you've just bought winter fuel, or are saving towards a large expense later in the year. But you could just as easily find that you have blown out your Spending Plan and need to fix it.

There are several ways to monitor your spending:
- Each time you enter something into your books, you assess the validity of the purchase. It's not a particular step you have to take, it's something you do by instinct. To use the winter fuel example, you might think

- As you reconcile your books, you'll see your expenses change month to month across the seasons. While it's fresh in your mind decide whether the variation is reasonable. Maybe take an average across the season or examine the differences between them.
- Compare a single item against departmental and total spend; does it feel too much for the return you got?
- Are there any strange money leaks that need plugging?

This is also the time to link your spending back to your vision and goals. Ask yourself whether each payment and purchase took you closer to where you want to be.

Did your emergency lunch Kit Kat bring you towards a healthier lifestyle? Did that glossy fashion magazine meet your Education virtue? Are you spending too much money on clothes when you wanted to save for an international vacation?

Controlling Your Spending

There's no point monitoring your spending if you aren't going to control it. That's like parking your car on a hill without applying the handbrake and watching it roll back down without trying to stop it crashing into people or other vehicles.

This is where you start *choosing* how to deal with runaway expenses according to your vision and virtues.

To go back to our monitoring examples, you may opt to keep healthier snacks at work, so you aren't tempted to visit the vending machine between meetings. You might decide that your fashion magazine was bona fide research for your winter wardrobe, but in a different context, you might download some books to read on your phone instead.

You might have accidentally side lined your vacation and have to refocus. Or you may have been promoted (yay!), abandoned your vacation, and are buying new work clothes.

In which case, you should recast your Spending Plan.

Sometimes it's easy to watch your spend creep up without taking any concrete action to stop it. To avoid this, you must set some relevant indicators to trigger further action.

For example, if your electricity bills are 5% higher than your Spending Plan allows for, you will investigate why. And then you'll use that information to choose an appropriate course of action.

If it's a seasonal variation, it should balance out over the year, and you need do nothing. But you might like to add successive levels of control.

If the bills reach 6% higher, you'll reduce your consumption. At 8% you'll find a cheaper supplier. Or at 10% you'll reduce your clothing spend to make up the difference.

You could also call these controls contingencies, or plans to deal with potential risk events.

Contingencies deal with possible but less predictable events like losing your job or your house burning down.

Events like price increases (e.g., rent and utilities) are predictable, which is why I encouraged you to include an allowance for inflation in your Spending Plan. There's more coming up on this in Chapter 12: Managing Risk.

Sometimes, controlling your spending means you need to change your habits, for example bringing water from home rather than buying it while you are out. Other times you have to change your expectations, like borrowing books from the library instead of buying them.

At some point, you may have to consider how to increase your income as well as cut your expenses. The list of potential controls is infinite, you'll need to do some research to determine which are best for you.

Let's take another look at the families.

Baker

Emily's priority is saving her apartment rental each month. Any slippage implies an inability to pay her rent, so this is a significant concern. If her savings are slipping, she needs to choose between a reduction in the quality of apartment she wants or adjusting her spending so she can save more.

She might notice that she's been going out with her friends a lot and choose to socialise less, or suggest that sometimes they stay home for pizza. Or if she notices she's made a lot of impulse clothing purchases while buying lunch, she might bring lunch from home to avoid the shops.

Emily enjoys making jewellery; chandelier earrings are her speciality. She has made a lot and could consider selling them as a side business to bring in a little extra income. She's making them anyway, but there's a cost in time and money to set up a market stall or list them on a craft site like Etsy.

Smith

The Smiths are focused on relocating. Their research program might involve additional costs that they haven't planned for, like phone calls, internet access, magazines and other research materials, plus trips to scout out potential locations. They may be noting these as incidentals and when they realise how much it's costing choose to recast their Spending Plan to make a particular department for it.

Some of these additional costs could have come from existing provisions in their operating costs, but others like the travel would be from savings. As the move will be in the new year and may involve a different climate, they might choose to cut back their clothing spend rather than buy clothes (or shoes) that may not work in their new location. They could also start pulling back on some of the local groups and activities they are involved with.

While Amanda does make a lovely cake, the costs (in time and money) of making them on a commercial basis are unfeasible. However, as they are planning to move, they can start decluttering and selling off some of the possessions they don't believe need to come with them.

Butcher

The Butchers are starting to think about a potential future where they aren't working. They're planning activities to reconnect with each other, and improve their health. They can enjoy these now, as well as expand them to fill uncommitted time in the future.

These are also relatively inexpensive activities in comparison to frequently going out for drinks and meals with friends and colleagues. They might find that they are spending less than expected and can divert these funds towards their retirement or travel savings. This is a useful thing to note, as it indicates that they may find it easier to transition to a more limited retirement income.

At this point, they don't need additional income, but it might be useful for them to consider what they could do to supplement their retirement. This might be looking for a business they could run, or starting to invest in products that will provide income.

Summary

Planning your spend won't help unless you monitor and control it to stay within the plan.
- Record your expenditure.
- Keep an eye on it to see whether you're sticking with the plan.
- If your spending starts veering off course, work out how to get back on track.

CHAPTER 5

Annual Review

You started this process with a vision, mission and some virtues, then developed some goals to bring your vision to fruition.

You developed a Spending Plan and started checking whether you were spending money consistently with your virtues in pursuit of your goals. You might have chosen to change your spending to get there quicker.

It's good work, and you could continue this approach and reach your goals on schedule. But life's not that predictable, and you have to stop now and again to take stock.

For most of us, this is around where we came in; New Year's Eve, champagne in hand, wondering where the year went and what we achieved.

Businesses also end their year with a review. They assess what went well and what not so well, take stock of their financial position, and start planning for the next year.

Statement of Net Worth

In business, a balance sheet is a statement of the difference between assets and liabilities. It supplies critical profitability information to shareholders and creditors, and is often all they have to gauge the likelihood that their investment will be repaid. Similarly, when you own stock, you probably want to know the business is making you money.

Like balance sheets, Statements of Net Worth are traditionally made up at the end of the fiscal year, but you can make one up whenever you want to know your situation is. For example, whether you can afford to buy a house, lease a car, or are better off than last year.

Figure 6 shows an example Statement of Net Worth. You fill in your assets and liabilities (debts), then deduct your debts from your assets to reveal your net worth.

DATE	Amount
Assets	
Current Assets	
cash on hand	
cheque/transaction account(s)	
savings account(s)	
Fixed Assets	
real estate	
car(s)	
jewellery	
art	
antiques	
furniture	
Income Producing Assets	
stocks	
bonds	
deposits	
funds	
retirement savings	
Other Assets	
loans to family/friends	
life insurance surrender value	
Total Assets	
Liabilities	
Short-term Liabilities	
Credit card(s)	
Store card(s)	
Overdraft(s)	
Tax(s)	
Outstanding bills	
Long-term Liabilities	
Mortgage(s)	
Car loan(s)	
Investment loan(s)	
Student loan(s)	
Loans from Family/Friends	
Other loan(s)	
Total Liabilities	
NET WORTH	

Figure 6: Sample Statement of Net Worth

The example is somewhere for you to start; some or all of it might not be relevant to you right now. Some line items (e.g., student loans) are more likely early in your life, and others (e.g., antiques) later, or not at all.

Some of your liabilities will also be assets. For example, the market value of your house may be an $800,000 asset at the same time as it is a $500,000 liability (your mortgage). Some of your liabilities (e.g., credit cards) are just debts. The main thing is to capture *all* your assets and liabilities.

The result could be a:

- **Deficit:** you owe more than you have in assets.
- **Surplus:** money left over, or more assets than debts.
- **Break-even:** your assets exactly balance your debts.

You compare this with your goals, to see if your financial performance was better or worse than you planned.

A deficit result can be quite shocking, but this gives you the opportunity to form a strong vision of a debt free future and formulate a plan to get there. The steps you take will be a combination of long-term strategy and short-term tactics that increase your assets and decrease your debts.

In the long-term you'll develop savings and investment plans (see Chapter 8: Saving Money) and manage your debt (see Chapter 11: Borrowing Money).

In the short-term you'll look in your account book to see where you can cut costs, find cheaper suppliers, or make bargain hunting a game and look for the least expensive items.

It could be many years before you break even or achieve a surplus, especially if you have a lot of debt (and if you went to University or bought property you probably do).

Bear in mind that debts can only reduce to $0, whereas assets (e.g., investments or real estate) have unlimited growth potential. You don't have to choose between paying down debt or buying assets – you can do a little of both at the same time.

The fact of a surplus is more important than a loss. A surplus that goes into saving, sharing or better food, clothing and housing will also provide a useful social return.

But, the temptation of a surplus is to put it towards stuff like flashy new cars and houses or fritter it away impressing others rather than saving and investing it to reach your goals faster.

Or cutting back across all categories to live an independent life funded by your investments.

General Review of Affairs

As well as drawing up your Statement of Net Worth, you should also review your:

- Vision, mission, and virtues to make sure they still reflect your needs and opinions (see Chapter 1: Vision, Mission and Virtues).
- Goal achievements; refine or set new goals and recast your Spending Plan accordingly. This will be much easier in the new year because you spent this year monitoring and controlling your spending and have all your records to hand (see Chapter 2: Goal Setting).
- Credit reference files to ensure there aren't any fraudulent additions. The quality and cleanliness of your file impacts your ability to access credit at reasonable terms so if any records don't relate to you, start the process of having them removed as soon as possible (see Chapter 12: Managing Risk).
- Household Inventory, to ensure all disposals and purchases are included and you have an accurate record of your belongings (see Chapter 6: Record Keeping).
- Investment philosophy and portfolio to see if any changes are required. Even if you only have a little money to put aside, it's worth taking a long-term view

about how you can grow it within your virtues framework (see Chapter 8: Saving Money).
- Risk Management Plan to ensure anything new has an action plan. And your insurances to make sure your coverage still meets your needs; not just the house and car, but life, health care, income, disability and long-term care (see Chapter 12: Managing Risk).
- Will and estate arrangements to make sure any changes in your family and circumstances (births, deaths and divorces) are included in your arrangements. As your financial affairs start getting more complicated, it may be worth visiting a lawyer who specialises in deceased estates to make sure your arrangements are best for you and your beneficiaries (see Chapter 20: Estate Planning).

I find the annual review is the most powerful part of the cycle. Even if you underestimated the difficulty of achieving your goals, you have moved closer to them and can celebrate.

Knowing you chose to take control of some aspects of your life and made a difference is tremendously satisfying, empowering, and inspiring.

It's also very comforting to see your debt reduce, your savings increase, and the life that you want coming closer rather than receding further into the distance.

Summary

Every year, check in with yourself to see how you're doing.
- Calculate your Net Worth (assets minus liabilities).
- Review your general affairs to ensure they are up to date with your net worth.

CHAPTER 6

Record Keeping

I'M AFRAID THAT WHETHER YOU'RE a person or business, there's no escaping the filing.

And regardless of who or what's doing it, the records must, as a minimum be accurate, true (reliable) and easily accessible.

Whether it's utility bills, purchase receipts, or the recipe for Nigella Lawson's chocolate brownies, looking for records can waste a lot of time.

You don't need a large bank of filing cabinets, just a simple box of index cards or an app will do for most records, as long as the location is easily accessible and you consistently file your papers according to the process you design.

Try to resist the temptation to use a bunch of different apps, books, boxes or cabinets; the important part of your system is that all the records you need are in the same place and you know where to find them.

Your initial set of records may be quite small, but as time passes it will increase, so you should choose a format that can expand as your needs and family circumstances change.

Additionally, there will be paperwork, and if you don't want to scan and save it electronically, you'll have to create a system to file it so you might as well, for the sake of convenience, use that for all your records.

This does sound complicated and time-consuming, but you're doing it already, just not systematically. It's the system that makes information retrieval quick and easy.

One way to be more systematic is to set aside space for an "office". Even if that's just a shelf and a drawer for records.

Like your vision work and departments, your record categories will be unique to you. And the easiest method is to grow and use the same categories across all your affairs.

You might like to develop your own system based on your virtues, as I did. Or this year's goals, or opportunities for further development. My friend Katy trained as a librarian, and uses the Dewy Decimal System!

Regardless of the method you use, you should make it very easy to locate the information that you need. Categories you could consider are:

Household Records

Your records of making and spending money.

Finances

These are your administrative, accounting, and legal records, so you should keep them for as long as you think is necessary; until a debt is paid off, your tax return, the statute of limitations, or indefinitely.

They relate to housing, insurances, taxes, banking, bills due and paid, receipts and receipt numbers, clubs and so on.

You could use an A-Z file or perhaps batch them and keep with your account books.

Important Documents

It's worth setting up secure off-site storage for important records and legal documents that would be difficult or expensive to replace. Papers like birth, adoption, marriage or citizenship certificates. Also, passports, property deeds, stock certificates and your will.

This is usually a bank safety deposit box, often in a climate controlled, fire and rodent proof secure storage room. Do note where it is located and what it contains in case other people need to access it, for example, for disaster recovery when you are killed or seriously injured (see Chapter 12: Managing Risk).

Safety deposit boxes come in different sizes, so pick one that can also contain any significant jewellery or other valuable items as well. You could also include a thumb drive containing copies of your records.

Household Inventory

You probably don't know the extent of your belongings, or what their replacement cost would be, so take and maintain an inventory. In its simplest form, the inventory is just a list of all your household goods.

It doesn't include fixtures like furnaces, only the furnishings that you own and can take with you when you move. You might find it easier to work room by room to produce a valued list for each one.

The inventory doesn't usually include items that aren't in the house, (e.g. your safety deposit box) but you could list them in a separate section for the sake of convenience.

It's mainly used for insurance coverage and claims, so include the purchase and disposal dates, serial numbers, repairs and maintenance details for each item.

For valuable items like antiques and jewellery, include a market valuation and a photo.

Don't forget your clothing and linens because they won't be cheap to replace. Depending on the terms of your insurance policy you could just estimate their replacement cost.

You might also like to note who you want items to go to when you die (see Chapter 20: Estate Planning).

Review your inventory annually, adding new items and deleting ones you've disposed of. Consider keeping a copy off-site with your other important documents (it's not useful if it's in the house when it burns down).

Library Records

These are your lendable collections of stuff like books, CDs, DVDs, sheet music, and sewing patterns. They could be items you own, want to read, buy or have loaned out, and want back.

Purchasing or Storage Records

This is partly for your Purchasing Plan (see Chapter 7: Spending Money), partly for determining quality and durability, and partly for ensuring the adequacy of your supplies.

It could include the preserves you make (date made, jars on hand, and the date used or disposed of). Or similar records for bulk pantry stores to help you estimate your shopping and how long things last in your house, for example, that you use half a pound (225 g) of coffee a week.

You might also monitor the brand, purchase date and cost of your household items.

Household Decoration

Details like room sizes, paint and wallpaper colours.

Household Hints

The articles you snip from magazines with the intention of trying, but lose before you do. For example, cleaning techniques and appliances to investigate or try, recipes, and garden plans.

Family Records

This is information about the people in your household.

Personal Information

For example, clothing sizes, where seasonal clothing is stored, and what needs replacing. When extended family birthdays are, the gifts you gave (to avoid duplication), and if you are a re-gifter, the gifts you received (so you don't give them back).

Medical Records

Records for each family member; practitioners, medications, test results, vaccinations, surgeries, and infections.

Keeping these up to date ensures that treatments like vaccinations are administered on time, and may provide early warning of the development of conditions like diabetes and heart disease.

They're also useful when you visit a new medical practitioner, or your children change schools, and you need to provide information about your/their health

You could add a tooth chart from your dentist and track your fillings, which need to be replaced around every decade. Plus, the date of your last eye test and your prescription.

Other Records

Addresses

All your contacts from everywhere. You could also note details such as spouses and children, anniversaries, favourite snacks and so on. Not just people, services such as utility providers, emergency tradespeople, the poisons information centre too.

First Aid

Instructions and treatments for common injuries and poisonings in your medicine cabinet. Review at least annually and discard/replace expired items.

Crafting

If you are a sewer, knitter or another type of crafter, a box and filing system for your patterns and materials.

Cooking

Your clipped and swapped recipes. You can categorise them however it makes sense to you; by ingredient, by meal type, by occasion, by kind of eater. Just remember to try each recipe first to see if it's worth keeping!

You'll probably use this collection a lot so you might like to keep it in your kitchen. If you punch holes in the top of each card, you can hang them on a hook as you use them, or stick a paper clip to the front of the box so you can use it as a recipe card stand, to reduce the chances of cooking messes.

If you don't want to stick them on cards, you could use boxes or envelopes instead, or transcribe them into an app. Regardless, your recipe file should be as reliable as your other household records.

Summary

Create a records management system that allows you to store all your records in the same place, and retrieve them quickly and easily.

- Set up secure off-site storage for important documents and items.
- Review and update records at least annually.
- Enable disaster recovery access for others

PART TWO:
Managing Money

THIS SECTION EXPLAINS THE THREE core components of managing wealth:
- Spending,
- Saving, and
- Sharing.

CHAPTER 7

Spending Money

WE'VE COME TO THE SOMEWHAT paradoxical part of managing money.

Money is the thing you get in exchange for pieces of your life, and in return, you spend it to get more life. Or at any rate, different bits of life; like a game of golf, a piece of chocolate cake or a new clothes washer.

I suspect that you not only don't notice your time passing, but you also don't see that you are spending it as well.

Unless you make an effort, you can go for days without touching any hard currency.

Your employer puts your pay into your bank account, your bills come out automatically, and you use a small plastic card (or your phone) at a bright beepy electronic machine to buy your groceries.

To get back in touch with the value of your money, you need to start touching it again; experience its smell, and texture in your hand. Taste the emotion of putting some into another person's hand and seeing how little remains in yours.

It may not be practical to take $1,000 cash to the store for your new washer (though you would really feel that transaction taking place), but you can gain some insight from paying cash for your cake or golf.

Give yourself a business-like petty cash float (or pocket money). Keep it in a beautiful new wallet with your notes sorted in order of denomination, all lined up the same way. Don't add any grubby old receipts or loyalty cards you don't use. Resolve to keep your wallet neat and organised.

Work out what's a reasonable float for you (based on your Spending Plan), and top it up each week. For comparison, here's what our families might do:

Baker

Emily may not need more than $100 for her morning coffees, the odd lunch and an after-work drink.

Smith

Amanda might need $300 for child and household incidentals, as well as pocket money for the kids.

Butcher

Ash and Jo may have been carrying $500 each, but drop it down to $250 to bring their focus back home to each other.

How Businesses Spend Money

In business, only appropriately trained and experienced people are permitted to negotiate purchases.

It's part of their job to continue their purchasing education and keep up-to-date with the market conditions that could impact pricing.

An experienced agent, guided by the organisational vision, mission, values and goals will save the business lots of money by planning purchases.

To make the process as efficient as possible, they develop a Purchasing Plan. The plan ensures the right materials are bought in the right quantity and quality at the right price at the right time.

The best time to buy is not so early you have to store and maintain the goods, but not so late you have to halt production.

The Purchasing Plan focuses chiefly on price, but the purchasing agent negotiates prices and delivery dates according to the strategy most likely to meet the business goals in keeping with its vision.

Put like that, it may not make a lot of sense, but if it's a business dedicated to child welfare, it's not going to knowingly buy products manufactured by indentured children in toxic environments.

Your Role as Purchasing Agent

From the perspective of a modern household, it's more important to know how to spend money than save it, and this means you may need to acquire new skills and knowledge.

Spending is a science, based on your virtues and living standards. You develop a straightforward and sustainable standard that works for the life you lead, instead of copying other people (e.g., the Joneses. Or some big-name celebrity).

As the purchasing agent, it's your responsibility to:
1. Maximise value and reduce waste by choosing brain, brawn, or money as the most appropriate purchasing medium, according to your vision and virtues.
2. Consider the additional costs such as deliveries, interest charges, and returns.
3. Evaluate the time and effort required to maintain the purchases, in line with your standard of living.

This sounds a bit abstract, so let's imagine you're a philatelist (stamp collector). Over time you have learned a lot of information that helps you separate good quality stamps from poorer. You know how best to store them to preserve their value. You have an idea of what they should cost, where to get the best prices and you've developed relationships with those dealers. There's a lot of other detailed knowledge too.

This is exactly the sort of knowledge you need to start developing about your Spending Plan departments.

Developing Your Purchasing Plan

Your Purchasing Plan consists of twelve calendar months, and takes account of major impacts on your spending including:

- Important dates, (e.g., birthdays, events like weddings, and other celebrations).
- Other calendars you use, (e.g., academic, religious, or sporting).
- The seasons.

To get started, you'll need your Spending Plan, some sticky notes, and markers. I suggest starting with sticky notes because they're easier to see and move about than a fixed width screen or calendar.

Plus, it's more fun!

As shown in Figure 7: Purchasing Plan, start by laying out a post-it for each month, and add the relevant information from your calendars. Then start thinking about the seasonality of your Purchasing Plan.

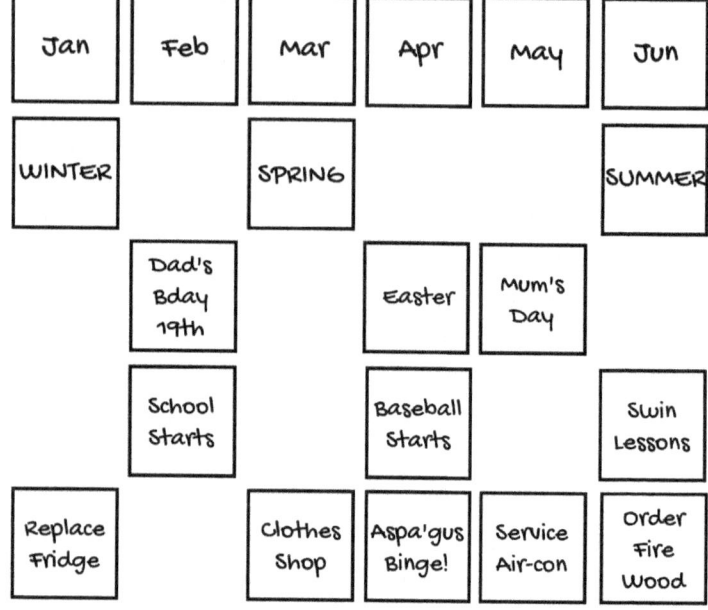

Figure 7: Purchasing Plan

For example, clothing comes in two major seasons (Spring/Summer and Autumn/Winter). The stores start changing stock around March and September, so if wearing the latest fashions is important to you, mark this period clothes shopping time. Or if bargains are more important, mark the main sales periods instead.

Do a little local research to find out when your best sales and buying times are for other items like linens and homewares, and note these on your calendar as well.

There are other logical times to buy; mid-summer is the most cost-effective time to buy winter fuel (if you have space to store it).

As fruit and vegetables come into season, they get cheaper. The further they travel the more expensive they are.

It's a good idea to schedule the maintenance and services of your fixtures before you need them, for example, your air-conditioner before summer, and your heating before winter.

While you won't need to replace your refrigerator every year, you might like to schedule major appliance replacement. If you buy them all at the same time, they may all need replacing at the same time, so try to schedule them for different years within their estimated life spans.

This also gives you time to compare prices or research the features and benefits of different models.

Once you've got it all down, you can start setting reminders and due dates in your calendar or diary app. Give yourself a month's notice for birthdays, or two for ones that need to be posted. If you know exactly when payments are due, you can put them in the calendar too.

You could leave it at that, or you could adjust your Spending Plan to match it. The Purchasing Plan in Figure 7 shows clothing shopping in March, so you would reduce your Spending Plan clothing allocations in other months to increase provisions for March. And the same across all your months for all your planned purchases.

It's perfectly fine to start by averaging your expenses out across the whole year because you'll probably forget to include something(s) in the first year. Your second year will come from your account book spending records.

Growing Your Knowledge and Experience

Price is not always the best indicator of value. Qualities like speed, durability or sustainability may be more important.

To become the best purchasing agent you can be, you need to know a little about business, politics, government, health,

labour, society and the relationships between them. You also need to know facts like:
- What your version of quality looks like.
- Manufacturing wages and employment conditions (e.g., occupational health and safety).
- What the costs of selling goods are.
- If the quality looks about right for the time and cost of production.
- Whether the price is appropriate for the seasonal availability of goods.
- Whether the price reflects efficient and effective production (or implies waste and disorganisation).
- The difference between price and value, and the importance of cost per use.

The best way to develop purchasing skill is to start where you are and consciously experiment:
- Consider the value, quality, durability and future investment of goods. Start keeping records to track these characteristics.
- Learn something about nutrition, food labelling, and the health impacts of additives and preservatives in food products. Understand the impact of food handling and manufacturing legislation, particularly when it comes to faults, errors and contamination.
- Learn about the properties and manufacture of fabrics, cookware coatings, cleaning products, and other items you use regularly.
- Understand the differences between trademarks, labels, advertising, product sizes and so on.
- If it's one of your virtues, join and work with organised buyers or advocacy groups.

How Your Virtues Apply to Purchasing

As a consumer, you and your virtues have an important part to play in issues of social justice and a sustainable environment.

Your choices directly impact the wages and working conditions of the people who make the goods you buy, and the social and environmental decisions made by manufacturers.

For example, Bisphenol A (BPA), is a chemical used to manufacture or coat food storage containers as well as some dental products.

It is a known endocrine disruptor that leaches into the food it contacts, so many countries have imposed "safe limits" on it.

Community lobbyists raised its profile, which increased media coverage leading to greater community concern. Legislative change followed, and now manufacturers label their products BPA free.

Conversely, your ongoing support of brand manufacturers can help them survive in an increasingly competitive global market based on cheaper, lower quality goods. Those who cannot compete may reduce quality to remain price competitive or go out of business (a lose-lose situation for you).

Understand that when you drop your standards, the market drops theirs too.

What to Buy

At some point, you're probably going to have to buy everything, so it's worth developing a purchasing policy or framework to guide your choices. Consider whether:
1. You need the item or not, followed by whether you'll use it often enough to recoup the cost. Don't buy tools unless you expect to use them frequently over an extended period of time, making cost per use, not purchase price your primary concern. For example, an

expensive toaster used daily will provide better value than a cheap waffle iron used only a few times a year. For more expensive items you could include the amount of interest foregone or charged as well as depreciation over the life you expect it to have.

2. The item will perform its task adequately for its life and is compatible for use with the rest of your equipment. That it's comfortable to handle and easy to use; pay particular attention to the ease and comfort of levers and handles, and their size, shape and location. Despite their low cost, flawed items ("seconds") are very unlikely to be useful or efficient tools due to their inherent flaws.

3. You can easily clean it; it shouldn't be harder or take longer to clean than to use. And you won't use it unless the end results are significantly better than otherwise. Can you, and will you take care of it properly? Will you have it serviced, get the blades sharpened use the correct detergent, and so on?

4. It has the most appropriate finishes for your goals. For example, is your non-stick pan the best for the food you regularly cook, or would you be better with plain aluminium, enamelware, or glass? Understand the requirements of your equipment and the differences between the models so that you will make the most efficient purchase.

5. It is a good fit for your life; will you make and eat fresh bread sufficiently often to justify a bread maker? Will it fit in the space you have prepared for it? Is it light enough for you to handle on your own?

6. Will it meet your needs; will you spend more time emptying than using the vacuum? Will the clothes washer/dryer take all your bedlinen in one wash?

Only once all these boxes have been ticked can you start considering its attractiveness.

Bulk Buying

While bulk buying can save money, it costs in other ways. You need adequate storage space, knowledge of the best way to store for long-term viability, and how to deter pests. Plus, you need to spend time and effort maintaining your stores.

The best products to bulk buy are the ones you use a lot. But you need to know how long they will last before you can make informed choices about how many to get.

For example, if you know it takes you three months to use a bottle of spray cleaner, and you have the opportunity to buy a crate of 24 (at a very generous discount), you can decide whether you want, and have the room to store six years' worth.

If it was something perishable instead, (e.g., coffee) you'd also need to know whether it would still be viable after that period of time, and so on. You might not want 24, but three for the price of two could be a more reasonable purchase.

Where to Buy

Your choices about where and when to shop have a wider impact than you might expect, so consider that when you buy too.

The first thing to think about is whether it may be more efficient to hire someone to shop for you.

Shopping costs you more than just the product price. It costs you time and effort getting to the store, shopping, and getting it all back home and put away. Not to mention the time spent looking for "bargains".

And if your time is better used to generate income, it costs you lost income too.

These days having someone else shop for you is more likely to involve subscribing to a delivery service or ordering online than hiring an actual person to shop for you.

When you shop yourself, you'll find the retail distribution chain has four major pathways:

1. Producer/grower sells to manufacturer (e.g., pea farmer to a producer of frozen goods).

2. Manufacturer sells to small wholesaler or retailer (e.g., a warehousing supply facility or supermarket chain).

3. Small wholesaler sells to a retailer (e.g. your local greengrocer).

4. Commission merchant buys from grower and sells to retailer (e.g., restaurant supply, wholesale market or your subscription service).

You can buy from any link in the chain.

In practice, your preferred perishables and necessities probably come in conveniently sized packages from convenient places closer to the end of the chain than the beginning.

And you're probably happy to pay extra for that convenience. You may prefer it that way because you can see and feel the individual quality whereas you might not in other links.

You pay distribution costs, for each link in the chain, plus an allowance to cover the risk that you won't buy at all. So, take this into account whether you are considering purchasing from the farm gate or the big supermarket.

The right place for you to shop balances the costs and benefits. For example, Emily picks up a couple of things at the supermarket on her way home because it's quick and easy. The Smiths might choose to take the children to the farm to see how food is grown, but the Butchers might use a subscription service because they live in the inner city and don't have a car.

Aside from time and cost, you might also like to consider your impact on the wider community.

Most of us have to choose between big company owned supermarket chains and smaller local retailers (owned and run by people like you).

You might lose time travelling to the big supermarket chain to save money, but the time saved shopping locally may outweigh the money saving.

In the longer-term, small local stores will close without customers, and you may be forced to travel as far as you must to the big company store.

And that might not be cheaper anymore (you may have already seen this where you live).

Small local stores depend on local shopper's repeat business and are more likely to provide personal attention and care as well as stock the reliable brands that sell consistently well.

Chain stores are primarily concerned with company profits, not quality or repeat business. They prefer to sell their own labels because they don't need to worry about product reputation, and they get to keep the profit that would otherwise go to brand manufacturers.

Summary

Your spending choices impact not just your bottom line, but also the stores that sell, brands that manufacture and workers that make the goods or provide the services.

Plan your purchases to achieve:
- the best value,
- the highest community impact, and
- the greatest efficiency.

CHAPTER 8

Saving Money

OVER THE LAST FEW YEARS, there's been a strange and vaguely troubling change in the meaning of saving money.

Where it once meant deliberately not spending money now in favour of a larger purchase later, it has come to mean buying goods at a reduced price.

Google "how to save money", and you'll find pages of tips for cutting your spending, but you won't find much that's useful for building a financial cushion or achieving your financial goals by not borrowing money.

This chapter is not about reducing spending, it suggests you change your definition of saving, and what it's for.

The word "save" has a lot of different meanings including:
- Thrifty.
- Redeeming (a saving grace).
- Reserving (e.g., dinner reservations).
- Reducing (spending or waste).
- An exception (everything but this).
- Respect (saving your presence).
- Protecting (e.g., life-saving).
- Salvaging (e.g., from a shipwreck).

The list goes on and on.

We've already talked about how spending money is exchanging pieces of your life for other pieces of life. In terms of wealth management, saving money is the opposite of this, it's accumulating life to use later.

One of my favourite authors, Terry Pratchett, wrote a book in which the secretive history monks use "Procrastinators" to save and redistribute small pieces of time. Taking it from the middle of the ocean, for example, and putting it in the midst of a busy city workshop.

While this rarely happens in money terms ("saving" when someone dies leaving you a legacy) this is kind of what you're doing by saving; stockpiling those grisly hours at work to be used later. Perhaps in Spain.

You've already developed a compelling vision of your future. You've set goals, and developed a Spending Plan to help get you there. Now I'm proposing you think of saving money as a way of nurturing your vision.

If Emily doesn't nurture her vision of living in her own apartment, it'll never happen. If Bob and Amanda don't cultivate their vision of a rural retreat, they'll be stuck in suburbia for years to come. And if Ash and Jo don't nurture their dream of travelling the world together, they'll be working until they drop dead.

If your vision isn't compelling enough to inspire your love and care, give it some more thought. At some point, you'll need to make some hard decisions, and your vision should give you the courage to make them.

If you find yourself a little perturbed about the notion of nurturing your vision because it involves taking care of money and therefore feels morally wrong, remind yourself it's not about the money *per se*.

The money is just a means to your end; it's your business class flight to Spain. It's a house with a garden big enough to camp out in. It's simply the way you get from here to there.

Developing Your Savings Plan

Money, like time, disappears when you don't prioritise its use.

Developing a Savings Plan is a lot like developing a Purchasing Plan, except you're not planning for a year, you're planning for your lifetime.

It's not just deciding to save an amount of money each month, though that's an excellent start, it's also giving your money purpose.

1. Pick Your Savings Accounts

If you have a business, you'll need at least one account for that to keep all your affairs (and business records) clearly separated from your personal (see Chapter 14: Owning a Business).

At the very least, you need one personal account to spend from, plus a separate personal account to save to (so you don't accidentally spend your savings).

Some advisers suggest a third account to hold your Spending Plan commitments before you spend them. There is some merit to this, especially since you'll have money designated for annual payments, and the balance could grow enough to need some investment thought of its own.

You could also open an account for each of your savings goals. However, the more savings accounts you have, the higher the cost of fees, and the less interest you'll earn, so consider whether you can control your individual savings goals through your account book.

Many banks and other financial institutions offer a high-interest product called something like a cash management account. They usually have conditions like a large initial deposit, or that you can't access your funds for a period of time (e.g., 30 days) after they are deposited.

Despite these conditions, they can be excellent places to park money in between saving and investing, and the perfect place for random income such as bonuses or tax refunds.

Some have benefits like cheque books, ATM cards, and lower fee structures than everyday accounts which also makes them useful for your Spending Plan commitments.

Alternatively, there are many kinds of online high-interest accounts accessible only by linking to an existing account.

Like any other kind of account, credit card or loan, you need to research which product is best for you right now.

And if you *need* the money, you can always close the account and take it back. Just don't forget to open a new account when possible!

2. Compound Your Interest

Compounding interest is the main reason you need to find the highest interest rate accounts that are practical for you.

The core concept is that by reinvesting the interest, you earn interest on interest, even if you never add another penny.

Say you invest $100 at 5% per annum (per year); at the end of the year, you have made $5 in interest.

- In the second year, you reinvest the whole $105 at 5% per annum, and make $5.25 interest.
- The third year you invest $110.25 and get $5.51.
- The fourth, invest $115.76 and get $5.79.
- The fifth $121.55 for $6.08.

After five years, your original $100 has grown to $127.63.

Okay, a return of $27.63 in five years isn't very exciting, but if you add an extra $100 each year as well, you'll have a return of $80.19 instead – almost three times as much.

That's marginally more exciting, but you probably won't see consistent returns over that period of time. The thing to remember is the process. A little bit over time, grows into a lot.

The earlier you start, the more your savings will grow. The more you put in, the more your savings *and* interest will grow.

3. Pay Yourself First

Your Savings Plan grows by paying yourself first; putting money towards your goals before you pay for anything else.

The easiest way to do this is to have your employer split your salary, with your expenses going into your spending account, and the balance to your savings.

Doing it this way, means any extra you get paid (e.g., tax cuts, pay increases, bonus payments) goes into your savings before you see it.

If your goals aren't big enough for dedicated savings, start with $5 or $10 (or even $1 if that's all you can spare) because something is better than nothing.

And it's always nice to have a little something set aside for emergencies or opportunities.

Make a commitment to save unexpected money (e.g., birthday gifts), as well.

4. Develop a Long-Term Strategy

Saving takes a really long time if all you do is put a little money aside each pay. Compounding your interest in a high interest account brings you closer to your big goals, but you can reach them sooner with a long-term strategy.

Your long-term savings strategy lays out the steps you're going to take, and when you're going to take them.

Like everything else you've done so far, it depends on what you're comfortable with, and that's subject to change over time. How much (or little) money do you feel you need to:

- Open a dedicated savings account?
- Start looking for a high interest account?
- Think about investing in funds and stocks?

This will vary according to the amount you want to save and how quickly you want to achieve your goals.

For example, if you want to save $100 in a year, you might just collect your loose change in a jar. Or for $1,000 in a year, you might open a dedicated savings account and deposit $83.34 each month.

So far, so good, but if you wanted to save more, say $10,000 but can't spare $833.34 a month, you might take a combination approach.

You could start by depositing $400 a month, and the loose change when the jar is full. When you reach $1,000, you transfer it to an on-call account with a higher interest rate. When that gets to $2,500, deposit it in a cash management account.

As your goals get bigger and your terms longer, you can add other elements to your mix. At $5,000 you might choose to invest in a managed fund. When you get $10,000, you might start buying individual stocks.

Investing in the stock market might seem terrifying right now, and it might be years before you get to that point, so don't start worrying about it until you're nearly there.

Focus on where you are right now, and as your savings grow, start thinking in more detail about your next step. Once you've opened a savings account, start looking for your high-interest account. And once you have that, look for an account the next level up.

Develop an Investment Plan

Investment is the big end of savings – the amounts are bigger, and the stakes are too. It's a bit scary, but it's what you do once your savings plan ceases to be the most effective way to maximise your returns.

I know developing an investment plan seems a little premature when you might have just opened your first savings account, but saving and investing is a long-term game. A small amount invested on a child's birth and managed well could pay for their college education.

Investment is the process of using your capital (cash and savings) to make a profit (return); you lend it to someone, and they return it to you with interest.

Investing can also be a way of contributing to humanity. If you lend money to a business (buy stock) it might build a factory, take on additional staff, or make better products to improve the lives of its customers.

This is not a book about investing, so we're just going to cover the basic philosophy and process. When you feel it's time, I recommend you seek professional advice.

These days, with low-cost online broking, you don't have to keep minimum holdings, and it doesn't have to cost a lot in fees. If it's going to be a decade or more before you need the money, you're cheating yourself if you don't.

If you're worried about stock, rest assured there are other options available to you. It's a good idea to start thinking some of this through so that you are ready when the time comes.

Get Started

Be aware that each investment you make is a gamble (even your choice of bank account); don't invest money you can't afford to lose – though you won't know whether you've lost money until you cash it in.

An individual stock might increase or decrease its return over the space of a year, but your risk reduces over five, ten or twenty years as the volatility is smoothed out.

If you're prepared to hold steady, the likelihood is that your investment portfolio will increase in value over the years you keep it; just like your home.

Especially when you reinvest your dividends (compound your interest) and average out your purchase prices (dollar cost averaging).

I once "lost" a lot of money because I sold stock to pay for my house deposit a few days after the market dropped (and of course it corrected a few days later). But despite that "loss" my return was still greater than my original investment.

Whether you trade yourself or through a broker, you need to learn the language of investing. Just like you have to learn the language of philately, blogging, or football when you start them. You can learn a lot reading blogs and joining forums.

Develop an Investment Policy

This will become a written document describing your philosophy, asset allocation and quality standards. It makes it plain to any financial advisers you might engage what your expectations are, and avoids misunderstandings.

If this makes you feel a bit bossy, remember that your vision of the future is at stake.

And you probably don't have a problem giving your yard service detailed instructions about what you want your garden to look like when they're done, so don't feel bad telling the people looking after your money what you want your investment portfolio to look like when they are done.

Philosophy
Your virtues are the core of your investment strategy.

You need to consider at least your lifetime, your potential partner, children, and grandchildren. By taking their needs into account, you're more likely to choose socially responsible or sustainable investments and, for example, avoid tobacco, armaments, or big polluters according to your virtues.

While you may not have enough money to invest directly right now, you can choose your banks and insurance companies according to the businesses they support.

You should also consider what your key investment strategy will be; income (low risk) or growth (higher risk)?

There isn't an objective right or wrong answer, it depends on what your virtues are and what stage of life you're at.

As a young person, you might favour growth over income and invest aggressively because you have time on your side. As you approach retirement, you may prefer more conservative investments that provide greater income than growth to spread your risk instead.

Taking into account how much time you can commit to managing your investments, you can decide how much to invest in stable low-risk options, and how much in high.

You could make a provision for experimentation too, perhaps 10% of your portfolio. And if you don't want to spend a lot of time on individual stocks, add some managed funds.

Asset Allocation

When you start investing you have to decide what mix of assets you're going to invest in.

A diversified investment portfolio spreads your risk across the three major asset classes; real estate, stock, and bonds.

Different asset classes do well in different types of economy, and if you've something like a third invested in each, you will always have some money doing well to offset the others.

- **Real Estate:** While you may not be able to buy property, you can gain access to it through a real estate investment trust or fund. Spread your risk by looking for different geographic locations and property types (e.g., residential, commercial, retail or industrial).
- **Stocks:** When you buy a stock, you are buying a share of a company. Ideally a mix of local and international, big and small companies, some with slow and steady returns to balance the more volatile stocks.
- **Bonds:** A bond is basically an IOU: you lend money to a borrower who agrees to pay you periodic interest, and return your capital on a given date in the future. The best way to manage risk is to avoid "junk" bonds,

and only buy government or highly rated companies that pay back within a five to seven-year time frame.

The right combination for you depends on your goals; how long you're investing for, whether you need the funds safe or can gamble with them.

For example, the investment allocation you make for your house deposit will be different to your child's college fund because you'll need the house money sooner and will be less prepared to risk it.

You may want some immediately accessible emergency money, and some less easily accessible for further investment purchases.

Table 1: Asset Allocation, shows what Capgemini found about how the world's wealthiest individuals changed their asset allocation to balance risk and opportunity in response to market changes according to its *World Wealth Report 2017*.

	2013	2016
Cash	28.2%	23.5%
Fixed Income	15.7%	18%
Real Estate	20.0%	14.0%
Stock	26.1%	31.1%

Table 1: Asset Allocation

Quality Standards

Your quality standards ensure you get the best investments managed by the most experienced people. While past performance is no guarantee of future results, good performance indicates a good team and suggests that future performance will be as well managed.

This does require you do some research and develop criteria for each asset you invest in. These might be standards like a minimum three-star rating from a research or rating agency (e.g., Morningstar), minimum price to earnings ratios, funds with a minimum asset base (e.g., $500 million), transparent governance structures, or financial strength.

Adviser Expectations
At some point, you may need someone to help manage your affairs. As well as your philosophy, asset allocation and quality standards you need to explicitly detail your expectations.

For example, that they will defer all decisions to you (or only those over a certain amount), fully explain tax implications, send you buying and selling transfer documents, monthly statements, an annual balance sheet and so on.

Choose Stock

Overall, your goal is to buy for less than you sell. Some stocks that seem expensive are well-established companies producing reliable dividends and don't vary much in price.

Others are very cheap because they're new unproven companies that might not survive, though if they do, could provide excellent returns many years later.

Over time, you'll find your portfolio loses its balance as the value of its components changes, or you buy too much of one and not enough of the others. You need to review it at least annually; reconsider your circumstances, listen to your gut, and buy and sell accordingly to re-balance it. (See Chapter 5: Annual Review).

Dollar Cost Averaging

The simplest way to start investing is by regular purchases of a particular investment, such as a managed fund: a process known as dollar cost averaging. When the price is lower, you get more units than when the price is higher, sort of like buying in the sales.

When you sell, you get the same price for all of them, making more profit on some than others, but receiving a greater overall return. This technique is used by most retirement savings plans.

Having said that, and bearing in mind investments seem more volatile over a year than a decade, you need to keep an eye on the market for confirmation.

If your stock or fund is going down when similar are stable or rising it might be time to swap it out for one of the others.

Trust Your Gut

Sometimes, making or losing money is more a matter of attitude or instinct than skill - some might call it risk appetite and others luck.

Regardless, if you don't feel good about some investments, then don't make them, no matter what others say.

It's a lot like those multiple-choice quizzes where your first gut instinct is the right answer, but before long you have reasoned yourself into another (incorrect) answer.

This is because your brain is always picking up all sorts of information you aren't consciously aware of, and when you make decisions, it draws on data you don't know you have.

Educate yourself and support your gut with research and sound reasoning.

If you aren't used to drawing on your gut, you'll have to learn to listen to it. Sit somewhere quiet and keeping your vision and virtues in mind, imagine different kinds of scenarios to see what feels right.

- Should you buy the stock your mate at the pub recommends?
- Should you guarantee your son's business loan with your house?

- Should you sell the blue-chip stock you inherited from Aunty Eglantine to buy that new tech start up?
- Should you relocate to another city for a job with the same income but fewer benefits?

These are important life changing decisions, and at different times and places in your life, you will get different answers.

You should always choose inaction over an option that fills you with dread.

If you're not sure whether your gut is reliable, start noting what it says, what you do instead, and how that works out.

- Should you have bought that stock?
- Should you have eaten the last cookie?
- Should you have serviced the furnace?

Not Getting Out

You also need to prepare to feel appalled when the stock market plummets. You're potentially watching your life savings disappear and panicking about when's the best time to cut your losses and pull your money out.

Work out how much capital you have to invest, how much you're willing to lose and convert that into a percent.

Brent Kessel offered the following investment ratio to guide your initial investments according to your risk appetite.

As Table 2: Investment Risk Appetite shows, if your risk appetite is low and you're not willing to lose any of your capital, allocate 80% of it to low risk fixed income assets.

If your appetite is high and you're willing to risk more than 30% capital, you could skip the low-risk investments.

Or somewhere in between, (like 20% of your capital), then put 20% into low-risk investments.

Maximum Loss You'll Accept (and stay invested)	Minimum % to allocate to cash investments
0%	80%
15%	40%
20%	20%
30%	10%
>30%	0%

Table 2: Investment Risk Appetite

You can also use these percentages as trigger points in your risk management plan to start selling.

If you're not sure where you fit in the risk appetite continuum, develop a recovery plan detailing the steps to get back up on one, if not both of your feet again should you lose everything (see Chapter 12: Managing Risk).

This is useful for two reasons:
1. You know your worst possible outcome and can make conscious decisions based on that.
2. You know exactly what to do if things go bad.

Sometimes being prepared is not enough and you'll want to sell no matter what. But before you do anything, try to understand and name exactly what you are feeling. Afraid? Determined to beat the odds? Overwhelmed? Sad?

Knowing what you're feeling will give you an idea of what you need to stay the course. Or perhaps just understanding what you feel and where the feelings come from will be enough to give you the confidence to carry on.

If you have a fee-based financial adviser, you could call them for advice. If your adviser is commission based, find a free one to call (to ensure that there are no conflicts of interest). If you feel you must sell, review your worse possible outcome and wait until you are calmer before you do.

Getting Out

It's always best to plan an organised asset sale. The closer you get to your goals, the more you should reduce your risk.

For example, with ten years to go before your child's college tuition is due, you could be as much as 75% invested in stocks, reducing to 50% at five, and down to 25% by two.

Keep your entire investment in safe and stable short-term bonds and money market accounts for the last two years.

Choosing an Adviser

If you don't want to manage your investments yourself (just yet), you need an adviser. And part of finding one is finding a reputable firm (bearing in mind the money and risk are still yours). You may get a free consultation, pay an hourly fee (with or without commissions).

The firm will allocate an adviser who should get to know you and your finances, goals and risk appetite so they can make appropriate recommendations.

When you meet them for the first time, take your investment policy with you to discuss. If you're in a committed relationship, take your partner and see if you get equal attention, and that the key terms and fee structure are explained clearly.

You should feel like they are trying to get to know and understand YOU as well as your financial position, and they want to offer the best advice for you.

Ideally, you'll share a long and respectful relationship.

But, regardless of their charm, or your feelings about the firm, remember you're there to make money. You need to understand the firm's experience and fee structure as well as the products you're thinking of investing in.

If you're in any doubt you won't make money, walk away.

You might like to think about hiring a female financial adviser. A 2009 research report *Women in Fund Management* undertaken by the National Council for Research on Women, suggests that women make better investors because they take a longer-term view and consider money and its impact on them and their families more holistically.

It's a means to their ends. So, they balance risk better, assess information that conflicts with their investment hypotheses, invest more consistently, trade less frequently (incurring fewer fees), have higher and more consistent returns.

Conversely, men are more likely to buy "hot" stock without research, invest too much money per stock, wait too long to sell, and trade too frequently. Men are also less likely to learn from their mistakes.

Minimising Fees

As with most things these days, investing involves fees. If you're not careful, they can cost your returns. And if you're unlucky, your capital too.

Additionally, some returns are subject to taxes which are paid before fees and can leave you even further out of pocket.

Choosing your adviser and investments carefully will go some way to minimising these costs, but if you can get the costs expressed as a percentage, you'll be able to compare this to your projected returns and make an informed decision about whether to proceed.

Future Proofing

With the long-term view in mind, you should start considering estate planning and tax implications; think about tools like family trusts or businesses to hold and divide your assets.

It's beyond the scope of my little book to advise you on this, so take local legal and accounting advice about how to protect your assets and minimise your tax and liabilities in both the short and longer term (see Chapter 20: Estate Planning).

Summary

Saving is the process of setting money aside now, to pay for things you want to do later.

- Developing Savings and Investment Plans gives you a roadmap to follow to meet your financial goals.
- Take a long-term view, and consider the effects on your potential partner, children and grandchildren
- Learn to trust your gut.

CHAPTER 9

Sharing Your Bounty

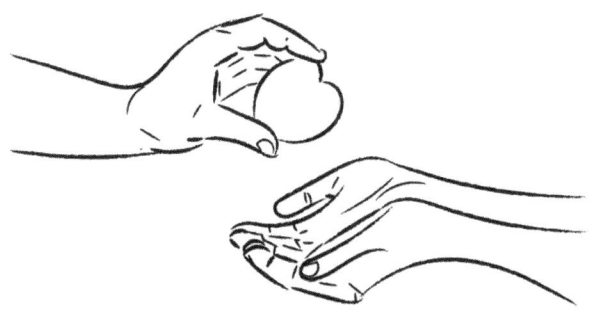

Your bounty is an abundance of something you have that others don't. Most people think of money, but it's the wealth we talked about earlier; time, brains and brawn as well.

When you feel wealthy you can relax, enjoy the people you're with, and feel compassion for others. You're more likely to share your wealth with those less fortunate than you, and when you do, it can come back to you, in unexpected ways.

Just as gratitude for what you have gives you compassion for others, making provision to share in your Spending Plan brings you a feeling of unity with them.

Your Spending Plan and account book reassure you there's enough to share, gives you the opportunity to act on your compassionate virtues, and the capacity to become something more than the sum of yourself.

It's human nature to want to be remembered for something, but we rarely plan for that. You're unlikely to meet anyone who came before your grandparents, and less likely to know much about them, how they lived, or what they cared about.

They may have built vast financial empires that were lost within two generations (as the majority are) because they failed to teach their children how to manage their money or make an impact on the world in which they lived.

Families like the Rockefellers who have maintained and grown their wealth have sharing programmes that focus on something larger than the family.

Setting up a sharing programme allows you to enjoy seeing the difference your donations make while you're alive, as opposed to knowing nothing about them because you're dead.

It also sets a precedent that may prevent challenges to donations made seemingly out of the blue in your will. And it teaches your children that your money isn't all about them; that you manage it for the benefit of all.

Why Share?

Giving a little something away makes you feel good because you did something good. You feel wealthy because you have enough to share, and are more grateful for what remains.

It's not just about the action of giving (though that's required), it's about the attitude of sharing.

Many faiths promote sharing to support others. Implicit in the encouragement to give is the acknowledgement of and permission to receive when you need to.

Don't be deceived by the part of you that says there will never be enough to share. When you give, you tell your god(s) you have enough, and you're willing to share it.

On the flip side, don't let your compassion and sincere desire to improve the lives of others, tell you that you have too much and must share it all.

Additionally, many governments outsource and underfund social services to not-for-profit organisations, who need all the help they can get.

Some governments offer tax benefits to incentivise donations, so you help yourself while you help them.

What to Share

Most people start with money, but sometimes sharing your physical strength, intelligence, or time are more useful. And often feel more worthwhile to share.

You might also give clothes, furniture and other ephemeral items that can be sold or used by others.

Some jurisdictions offer personal tax incentives including the fair market cost of investments and other assets, though you would be wise to check the specific provisions where you live and take the advice of an appropriately qualified accountant or financial planner.

When to Share

Sometimes you feel too poor to share, but this is the very best time to give. This is the exact time you might start feeling unworthy, collapse in on yourself and withdraw from others.

That feeling of unworthiness is what makes this the time to be courageous and reach out. If you don't have money, you probably have time and skills you can share instead (which might help you develop new skills you can earn from later).

Sometimes it takes the personal tragedy of someone you know to make you think further than yourself. You may be inspired to donate to medical research or start taking better care of your body and the people in your life.

When you feel compassionate is also the time to share, even if it's just for the tax credit or to be seen as a good person.

It's easy to be compassionate towards people you have affection or pity for, but less easy when it involves people you think are undeserving.

You have to train yourself to lay aside your judgements and understand they may need your compassion and friendship more than others.

How to Share

When you share, do it intentionally and with awareness of the possible ramifications.

While you might feel that you're selflessly giving with an open heart to someone you know, your chosen recipient might find it hard to take your gift with dignity and appreciation.

That mightn't sound like the people you know, but think about how they (or you) reacted last time you offered to buy them lunch or pay for a double date.

Did they gracefully accept your offer with thanks, or did you spend twenty minutes arguing about it before getting into a fist fight at the cash register?

Your friends could feel like a charity case with an implied obligation to you, and this isn't the outcome you want. Just like debt, it can destroy your relationships.

The purest way to share is anonymously, to causes you care deeply about. Or if you are inclined, put it in the hands of the deity of your choice by giving it to a spiritual group.

How Much to Share

While you shouldn't give more than you can afford, you should give enough to feel generous; it needs to *feel* worthwhile.

And if you want to give regularly, do it intentionally, early in the month as one of your priority items. If you can't make it a set amount, perhaps you could collect your coins and give them at the end of the month.

There are many recommended giving amounts ranging from 10% of your income to 1% of your net worth, but you need to decide how much is right for you in keeping with your virtues, goals and circumstances.

If you need to give more than 10% right now, do it. If you need to give less, likewise.

Who to Share With

When you consider organisations to include in your sharing programme, consider how much of your donations will reach the people you hope to benefit.

Service provision incurs administrative and direct service costs, but try to support organisations that are very efficient and minimise their administrative costs without sacrificing the health and well-being of their paid and volunteer staff.

The organisations you'll pick depend on your virtues. Don't be afraid to re-prioritise during your annual planning.

For example, you may become more concerned about Alzheimer's as your parents age and you take on more caring responsibilities for them, and less concerned about cancer as your brother completes his treatment and goes into remission.

Other people's priorities change too; as you move your giving away from cancer, someone will take your place, just as you take the place of someone leaving Alzheimer's.

Or other concerns like clean water, homeless shelters or women's refuges.

You could also consider investing through micro-finance; offering small loans to people with tiny businesses. You might finance capital investments like an oven, sewing machine or cow to help a business grow.

If the loan is paid back, you can lend the funds to someone else, if it isn't you haven't lost anything because you were planning to give it away anyway.

This might be something you could do with your family according to your virtues. You can select individual borrowers through an online lending platform like Kiva.org, or join an organisational process through a formal investment fund.

Summary

Sharing your wealth with others will help them, and make you feel good about yourself:
- Choose recipients in line with your virtues.
- Share enough to make if feel worthwhile.
- Share mindfully.

PART THREE:
Living with Money

THIS SECTION DISCUSSES SOME OF the financial considerations that come up at key points in most people's lives.

CHAPTER 10

Understanding Your Past

JUST LIKE YOUR TASTES IN vegetables and pets, your childhood sets the scene for your adult beliefs about wealth. Generally, these were appropriate for that time and place, but could be holding you back now.

Before we can look at how to deal with these beliefs, you need to understand the basics of how your mind works. To put it *very* simply, your mind has three parts.

1. **Your Conscious** is the bit you think of as "me". It's the Chief Executive Officer of your business issuing staff directives. It's aware of what you're doing, and does your thinking, reasoning, planning and so on.

2. **Your Subconscious** is your staff. It follows the CEO's directives, and does what it thinks is necessary to achieve what it thinks the Chief Executive wants. It remembers how to ride a bicycle, get home, and not burn your fingers on hot things.

   When it doesn't know what to do, it asks the unconscious for advice. But it's like doing an internet search; the answers don't always exactly match the question.

3. **Your Unconscious** is a big messy stack of everything you've ever seen, heard, felt or thought; including the traumas you've repressed and all the experiences you've forgotten. It's the source of your habits and gut instincts.

   Your conscious can't easily access it, (which is why it's difficult to resolve childhood traumas without professional help) but it can be triggered by smells, sights and sounds. Which is why you may still be terrified of thunderstorms, faint at the sight of blood, or remember your grandmother when you smell lavender.

Memories and Your Unconscious

As a child, you saw the extremes of emotion that wealth or its lack caused. You accepted the beliefs behind them as unquestionable fact; like money doesn't grow on trees or you have to work hard for it. And this led you to you make some resolutions about how you'd manage wealth when you got some.

These resolutions are the core of your beliefs about your place in the world; the one who doesn't like broccoli or the one who can't afford the new "in" clothes.

When your memories spark related emotions (good and bad), and when you feel like you need protection, your subconscious triggers and reinforces the coping behaviours you learned as a child.

In general, this is good, because it inspires you to take action. But, it's not so good when you're afraid and overreact, for example, by excessive frugality or binging on clothes or food.

Even seemingly happy memories, like the thrill of landing a good deal can trigger negative coping behaviours like gambling or workaholism.

These childhood beliefs are also your foundational beliefs about life and wealth, and you don't need to think about them.

They're just there in the background giving you a comfortable automatic fall-back position; you make yourself safe by putting yourself back in the place you believe you belong (e.g., the one who can't afford the new "in" clothes).

Whatever they are, your unconscious beliefs are usually selfish; taking care of yourself at the expense of everyone else.

It was ingenious of you to make those choices as a child, but as with all adult situations, unquestioned obedience to childhood conviction does not bring happiness (broccoli is a "super food" - you should try it).

Clinging to those attitudes is more likely to destroy all that you hope to achieve.

Maybe you're desperately trying to keep up with your wealthier friends, even though you're on the poverty line. Or you scorn them and their money, hiding that you're a thousand times richer.

Not only does this reduce the benefit of your relationships, but each time you unquestioningly obey your unconscious you reinforce its beliefs.

Regardless of how much you consciously tell yourself to stop spending and pay off your debt, it just can't happen until you understand why you spend.

Coming to understand those reasons is hard because it is as uncomfortable as questioning the fact of gravity. And your truth might be buried so deeply that you can't remember it without professional help.

Examining Your Unconscious

Just like breathing; the majority of actions you take are managed of by your subconscious so your conscious can focus on the important now stuff (like sabre tooth tiger spotting).

While your unconscious and unexamined beliefs and behaviours guide all your decisions across your whole life, the good news is that you can change them.

You just need to work out what it is that your unconscious (or inner child) needs; what makes it feel safe, what makes it happy, and what it desperately wants more than anything.

Which is nowhere near as easy as I just made it sound.

Your inner child isn't a separate persona that exists within you, it's a metaphor for the innocent and playful childlike part of you – the part that jumps up and down laughing and clapping when it hears good news.

So often in the rush to adulthood people stop believing in and taking care of their inner child; they put it away with Santa, the Easter Bunny and the Tooth Fairy and move on to more grown up ways of dealing with the mysteries of life like alcohol and other kinds of addictive behaviours.

There are many ways to get back in touch with yourself, but the most important one is to acknowledge that the child is still within you and that its desire for love, protection, and acceptance is as strong as it was when you were that child.

It's your job to take its concerns seriously and provide the reassurance it needs.

In terms of money:

- When a situation triggers a memory, take a moment to examine it. Decide whether the coping behaviour you feel compelled to complete is still useful, or is damaging your relationships, health or well-being.
- Observe your thoughts when you want to buy something. Choose to delay purchasing to see what memories and emotions come up. Make a note of the physical changes in your body when you think about the object - how does it feel to want it? Does the intensity change as the days pass; do you feel more or less fulfilled? Note how the changes feel as time passes, and how you feel if you go ahead and purchase.
- Translate your memories into the simplest language, for example; "spend money, feel loved". See if this makes it easier to understand and dissipate your feelings and coping behaviours.
- Take some time to think about your childhood wealth experiences, and compare how you felt then to what you would feel now. Details like the types and sources of your best and worst gifts and treats, the items you stole or were jealous of. How you felt about your

mother working (or not), the state of your home and possessions, having to work for your pocket money.

This isn't easy work, and I'm not a psychologist, so if you find this difficult, consider seeking professional support.

Changing Your Behaviour

Choosing to change is the easy part.

Identifying how your earliest or most painful memories about money motivate your unconscious behaviours is much more challenging.

But once you make that choice, you'll start noticing when your memories trigger actions.

It's going to be leopard changing its spots difficult, because you also have to face the fact that everything is not going to be ok exactly as it is. And your inner child will have tantrums and stamp its feet or hold its breath.

It can help to think of the memories in different ways:
- Review them like movies; look for plot holes, inconsistencies, and failures of logic.

    Would Jason Bourne *really* use his credit card to buy guns and ammunition? Once you review that movie, you move onto the next.

    Would Hermione Granger-Potter buy groceries at her local muggle supermarket with Gringotts gold?

    Don't feel you have to binge watch them; take as long as you need.
- As computer programs.

    Athletes whose careers rely on the perfect shot, swing or kick spend a lot of time visualising, hoping to program their minds and bodies on what to do.

When they make a less than perfect shot, they immediately overwrite the memory with their perfect shot visualisation.

When you trigger a memory, you can use this technique to imagine a new and better scenario of your adult self dealing comfortably and confidently with the triggering event.

- Like viruses. Just when you think it's gone; it mutates and comes back. It takes time and consistent conscious effort to fully eliminate them.

As you review your memories, keep the healthy and adaptive aspects that are appropriate for your life, but let the obsessive and unhealthy behaviours go.

At this point in your life, you do know something about money, and have a vision for your future.

To move towards that future is to bring your conscious and unconscious minds (mediated by the subconscious) into a balanced place where you can make choices informed by both.

You'll know when you've made this kind of balanced decision because you'll feel yourself let go of the weight you've been carrying. You'll feel relaxed, and deeply calm.

Well, once you've learned how to feel it, that's what you'll feel. You'll need to practice "pulling yourself together".

Remember that your conscious and unconscious minds are like political parties. They want the same outcome (e.g., happiness, security, or independence), they just disagree about what exactly that looks like and how you're going to get there.

It's hard work. It may be depressing or make you angry. But it's not about solving the world's problems, it's about bringing yourself into harmony with yourself.

Awareness is just the first step towards you becoming the person you're meant to be.

Fear

When you hide from fear, you give it your power. When you ignore it, it multiplies exponentially.

Fear of not having enough this month grows into fear of not having enough in general. Which explodes into fear of losing it all, then fear of having nothing which turns into fear of being nothing.

There's a HUGE difference between the starting and finishing points.

Having to delay paying a bill this month doesn't reduce you to nothing, but you'll probably remain financially powerless until you face the fear and take your power back.

Facing fear makes time and space for you and your wealth to grow.

Stop and think about your fears, like becoming a bag lady. Or not being able to get a job. Or that if people find out how much wealth or debt you have, they won't like you anymore.

They're probably connected to childhood events:

- Your belief that money slips through your fingers could relate to dropping and breaking something precious as a child.
- Your inability to trust a partner with a joint account might result from someone raiding your piggy bank.
- Your fear of a tax audit could relate to not returning an overpayment of change from the sweet shop.

If an action becomes apparent to you (like buying and using a precious thing or making a donation), do it and move on.

You might like to write the rest down and consider it further later.

While there are many ways to say no, you can only say yes from your heart. You're retraining your mind to believe that your money fears are untrue; that you *really* do deserve to do well, and that there *really* is enough.

Instead of learning to do without, you're learning to do with.

That you need money doesn't say anything about you at all – we all need money! You need to face your fear of not having enough before you can take control and replace it with more helpful and constructive beliefs.

Reframe Your Thinking

One way to retrain your thinking is with a positive and empowering financial affirmation or mini-vision. Create a tweetable, based on a minimum (e.g., at least $10,000 per month) and set in in the present (e.g., "I am" or "I earn").

Say it every time you look at or think about money; keep saying it until you are comfortable with it and can say it without cringing. Then say it some more.

Your fear will fight back, but just keep repeating your affirmation. Your new truth is bigger than your fear, debt and worries combined.

This won't do anything more than retrain your thinking. But, as you convince yourself that "I am a successful (insert noun here) making at least $10,000 per month", you start making choices that reflect this truth and bring it into being.

Alternatively, you could try afformations; essentially an affirmation in the form of a why question.

According to their inventor, Noah St John, asking why puts your subconscious into problem solving mode. It focuses on what's positive about you and your situation.

The why question also relates to your intention, and points you back towards your vision.

And when you're back in touch with that, you can move onto how (your method) and reconnect with your goals.

Another way to reinforce your thinking is to choose relevant and meaningful computer passwords. You might choose to confront a new fear or create a new belief each month. Login by login you will reinforce the new belief as you go.

Disclaimer

I'm not a psychologist, and I'm not licensed to give psychological advice. My definitions and suggested actions have been put into simple language which reduces the accuracy of my explanation. If you have any concerns at all, seek guidance and advice from a qualified and licensed professional.

Summary

Your childhood experiences control your automatic reactions to wealth situations. If you want to take control of your wealth behaviours, you need to:

- Understand your subconscious reactions.
- Deal with your fears.
- Reframe your beliefs.

CHAPTER 11

Borrowing Money

OFTEN, SPENDING MONEY INVOLVES BORROWING money. And if spending money is swapping bits of your life for different bits of life, then borrowing money is spending life you haven't lived yet.

Credit cards offer you an easy opportunity to spend the rest of your life before you've lived it.

You don't have to think about whether you need a thing, or even consider whether you *want* that thing. You just buy it.

And just as you have almost spent your full limit, your bank might offer you a top up.

When I was younger, and credit cards were a new and exciting thing, I was living the high life on an annual gross income of $25,000. I had a credit card with a limit of $55,000, and I had almost fully extended it.

When I received an offer to increase it to $63,000 (310% of my net income) I knew it was big trouble because I could buy a plot of land *and* build a house on it for that much money.

And that was not the only credit card I had.

That one credit card represented three years of my life, and of course, it took a lot longer than that to pay it off.

Debt

Credit cards are not the only form of debt. There's also the money you borrow from friends and family, back taxes, and maybe store credit too.

Some debts are "good" debts because they increase your net worth (e.g., a mortgage) or help you generate income (e.g., education or investing). Though you can't always be sure that those debts will bring you the results you hope for.

The rest is "bad" debt, mainly because it doesn't increase your wealth; debt like car loans and credit cards.

Then there's the avoid at all costs debt, like payday loans.

Consolidation loans are various shades of grey; you combine all your debts into one low-interest loan and repay it in instalments. Except that most people don't cancel the original debts and just spend it up again.

The money you owe friends and family corrodes your relationships. And saps your life of happiness because you start avoiding the people you love.

You worry they'll ask you about the debt. You're afraid they need the money more than you. And you can't do things like go out for dinner in case you see them.

If your debt gets as big as mine, and you're paying a huge interest rate, you might never pay it off. I paid 29% - an additional $15,950 every year the debt remained unpaid.

Compounding monthly.

That additional $15,950 in annual interest prevents you from achieving your goals; a house of your own, exquisite artwork, or developing an expensive foreign cheese habit.

It's well established that people like to keep company with people like themselves, people with conservative political views, people who smoke, people who go mountain biking.

And it's the same with credit providers.

Respect yourself and your money and choose your credit card company as carefully as you choose your babysitter.

Keep your limit low, and your interest rate the lowest. Use it carefully, and pay it off in full each month. Or as quickly as you can.

And remember that credit card companies are not your friends; you are their means, and their end is to get as much money out of you as possible.

If they offer you a "favour", examine the fine print carefully because it's more likely to be a trap to drag you deeper into debt than a foothold on the path out.

Developing Your Debt Reduction Plan

1. Write Down How You Feel

Before we start talking about paying down debt, take a moment to write down how you feel.

The dread gnawing at your guts, the weight of the world on your shoulders, the desperation of not knowing where your next meal is coming from.

This is the antithesis of your vision work, you need to describe your situation as vividly and explicitly as you can so that when you feel the enthusiasm of paying your debts off decreasing, you can reread it for extra motivation.

If your vision is the rewarding carrot drawing you on, this nightmare is the punishing stick that's driving you.

2. Destroy Your Credit Cards

The main way to get control of your credit card debt is to stop using them.

While you're still in the grip of your nightmare anti-vision destroy your cards before you can reason yourself out of it.

It's the ideal time to start using cash to get back in touch with the nature of your money.

These days you can't really get by without an emergency credit card. But emergencies DO NOT occur in fashion stores during sales.

They occur on streets in car crashes, during storms when the wind blows your roof off, or the middle of the night when you must fly cross-country for a family illness.

While it would be easy for me to say ONE card with a $1,000 limit, emergency limits are going to be different for all of us. Our families can show us how this works;

Baker
Emily is young and single. Even when she moves into a place of her own, she's unlikely to need more than about $1,000 to cover a car or appliance breakdown.

Smith
The Smiths might need as much as $10,000 in case Amanda has to stay in a hotel in the City while Daniel or Lisa is in hospital.

Butcher
Jo might need to fly cross-country to spend time with a dying parent. And as Ash travels for work, they might be better with separate $15,000 credit cards while they wait for the expense claims to be paid out.

3. *Work Out What You Owe*

Now that you've got rid of your cards, list all your debts:
- The amount,
- The minimum monthly payment,
- The interest rates, and
- Interest types (daily or billing cycle average).

Don't forget to include your friends, family, the tax man, and any others.

Your provider's minimum monthly repayment probably won't cover the interest and fees let alone reduce the debt. Check your statements; add up the fees and interest, and if that amount is more than the minimum payment listed, write that down instead.

Then go back and add an extra $10 to each repayment on your list so you'll feel like you're making progress.

Add all your repayments up to get your minimum debt repayment total.

4. Work Out What You Can Pay

Go back to your Spending Plan, and look at your income and spending again. While you still want to live a happy life in pursuit of your vision, the debt you're carrying is reducing your happiness potential.

Weigh up your vision, virtues, and goals against your nightmare anti-vision and consider where you might be able to cut your spending a little more to provide the largest sustainable amount you can afford to pay down your debts.

Deduct your total debt repayments from this amount. The minimum payments will maintain the status quo on the bulk of your debts, and the rest pays off each debt in sequence.

5. Pay Off Your Debts

There are many strategies for paying off debt:
- Highest interest rates first because they're costing the most money.
- Debts that calculate interest on the average balance because they cost more in interest.
- Clearing the smallest first for a quick win, leaving more to pay off the rest.
- Family and friends first to improve your relationships and increase your happiness.

It's worth considering a combined approach. If you have debts you can clear in the first few months, pay them off first.

Then recalculate the payments and put the bulk towards the highest interest rate that uses an averaging calculation.

Monitor the balances, and when they're low enough to knock off with one payment, make it and recalculate the payments again.

Don't forget to instruct the company to close the account. This is particularly important with fee-based accounts because the fees will continue even when the debt has been paid off.

Celebrate the discharge of each debt as you go, maybe include a ritual bill burning.

6. Write Down How You Feel

I cannot begin to tell you how exciting and exhilarating it is to see the balances come down, and your debts paid off (something else an account book is good for).

Once all your debts are paid off, take a moment to experience how that feels.

The tightness in your chest is gone. You can stand up straight as you are no longer bowed under the weight of the debt. You're walking a foot above the ground.

Take out the paper you wrote your nightmare anti-vision on, and on the other side, write how good it feels to be out of debt and your intention to never let it get that bad ever again.

Then when you're tempted to spend up big, choose whether the carrot or the stick is more likely to stop the spending craving.

Supplemental Remediation

Aside from paying off your debts, there are some little tasks you may need to do, depending on the extent and condition of your debts.

- If you're late or have missed payments, contact your lender and explain the situation. They already know you can't pay, and it will be easier to open negotiations with them before they start calling you. Let them know how much you will be paying and when.

- Check your credit reference file. If there are errors or inaccuracies, start the process of correcting them as they will affect both your credit rating and interest rates as long as the issues remain outstanding.
- Do some research and find the credit card that best meets your current needs; whether that's low fees, low rate, low minimum monthly repayment. If you plan to consolidate all your debts into it, make sure you understand how they calculate and charge interest on purchases after you transfer the balance. And if the same conditions apply to all transfers or just the first.
- Contact the companies you owe who are charging you the highest interest rates (that you are not late with repayments). Tell them you're thinking of swapping lenders, and details about the card you've selected and ask what they can offer you to stay. Sometimes they'll offer a better deal and sometimes they won't. If they don't, or it's not as good as the one you have identified, then close the card and move it.

Repaying Debt from Other Sources

You may think you're in a position to draw back from your retirement savings or extend your mortgage to cover the debt, but avoid this if possible. These are booby trapped quick fixes:

- If you don't change your spending habits and get rid of your cards, you'll quickly double your debt by running it up to the same limit.
- You'll give yourself a precedent. If you felt your circumstances were bad enough once, you'll find it easier to give yourself permission a second time.

Retirement Savings

When you draw from your retirement savings, you lose not only your savings but the growth that comes from long-term investment too.

You might never pay it back. If you do, you'll probably be using after-tax income to pay off a pre-tax investment. You'll have to pay tax on it when you retire and withdraw it; so, you'll be double taxed.

Your Home

When you use your home as security for a loan to pay off your credit card debt, you'll get it cheaper and possibly get some perks with it. But you may not have enough equity to pay off all your debts.

Additionally, you may have to pay mortgage insurance, which protects the bank if you stop making payments. The insurance company may take proceedings against you to recover their losses - you could lose your home but not your debt.

The only benefit to you is access to a loan the bank doesn't think you can afford.

It's also possible to get a line of credit secured by your home which is more or less a credit card with a limit the size of your home's value.

Neither the interest rate nor the payback period is fixed. If you're not disciplined, the debt will quickly spiral out of control as you continue the spending habits that got you here in the first place.

If you feel you have to take on a second debt to pay off the first, carefully research your options, just as you did to find a new credit card provider.

Consider the applicable interest rates and calculations, fees, repayments, and term to pick the one that best meets your needs at this time.

Make it your top priority to pay it off, or if this loan won't cover all your debt, add it to your list of debts and get it gone.

More Help

If you aren't able to make these options work, you need to get help. The best place to get it is through a not-for-profit financial counselling service.

They'll help you negotiate with your creditors, fill out any legal forms you might need, and teach you how to manage your money at the same time.

For a small fee, they may also pay your creditors for you, but make sure that you understand the fee structure, and organisational ethos as some organisations charge you for services you can do yourself for free.

And there's always the possibility that they're doing what's best for themselves, and their business, not for you.

Summary

Borrowing money is spending life you haven't lived yet.
- Some debts build your net worth, most don't.
- When debt gets out of control, you need to stop spending and make a plan to pay it back.
- Avoid using money already invested for your future.

CHAPTER 12

Managing Risk

THINGS GO WRONG ALL THE time, and usually we find ourselves saying "If only...".

Being prepared, and managing your risks gives you the opportunity to turn that around, and say "Thank goodness I...".

How Businesses Manage Risk

Risk management is another area where we can learn from business; they employ a Risk Manager to think about what might go wrong in the future and recommend steps to eliminate or minimise the risks and their consequences.

Plus, they think about what might go well, and how to maximise the benefits.

However, some risks and opportunities can't be identified until they happen because there just isn't enough information to see them coming.

Risks are events that have causes and effects. Some are more likely than others, while some have more severe effects.

Some are caused by the external environment (you can't control those), and others by your internal environment (you can control these).

Some events affect the broader population, and these are generally external events you can't do anything about.

Others affect just you, and these are usually internal events you can do something about.

Once a risk event happens, it becomes an issue and must be dealt with, so the Risk Manager develops a Risk Management Plan to deal with it.

The plan identifies the risk events, assesses their likelihood, the severity of their effects, and recommends strategies to manage them.

This gives you the opportunity to reduce the risks and effects, deal with the event at the time, and handle the recovery.

Your Role as Risk Manager

For you, risk management is about protecting your vision, mission and goals. Your virtues guide and constrain the actions you take to protect them.

You may find this chapter difficult because you'll be thinking about worst case scenarios including your death, the destruction of your property, and losing everything you love.

But I urge you to persevere so you can rest safe in the knowledge that you've done all you can to contain the fallout, and your preparations will minimise the damage.

I know it's not very helpful to say, but you're the one who knows best what your risks are.

They're the things in your life that give you nightmares; hurricanes, car crashes, having your home broken into, being assaulted in the street and so on.

You're also the expert on your local environment, you know who to call in an emergency, and the limits of your abilities.

All I can do is offer some thoughts to guide your process.

Developing Your Risk Management Plan

The first thing to do is to think about your life as it is, and as you want it to be.

Then write down every single thing you can think of that could go wrong and prevent you from getting there.

You don't have enough information to predict everything, but anything you can is a good start. You'll be reviewing the plan during your Annual Review (see Chapter 5: Annual Review) so you can update it as you think of new risks.

It doesn't matter whether the risks you identify seem small or unlikely, list everything that you can think of; for example, that a tree might fall on your home.

And if anything pops into your head about something that might go really well, write that down too.

Determine Your Events

Then, for each of those risks, write down all the possible causes that you can think of.

The cause of a tree falling could be a storm that blows it over, someone drives into it, or it's infested with termites.

As you run out of causes, start thinking about the effects; death or injury, the house is damaged, or you must move out.

Determine their Likelihood

Next, use Table 3: Risk Likelihood to give your causes a likelihood rating.

	The event...
Rare	will only occur in *exceptional* circumstances
Unlikely	*could* occur at some time
Possible	*should* occur at some time
Likely	will *probably* occur in most circumstances
Bound to	is *expected* to occur in most circumstances

Table 3: Risk Likelihood

For example:
- If the Smith's new property is partly forested, a tree might fall on the house during a storm. It would have to be a big storm, so the likelihood is Possible.
- The Butcher's inner-city apartment would need some kind of fantastical event to cause a tree to fall on their home, so the likelihood is Rare.

Calculate the Severity

Next, give each consequence a severity rating.

Holistic Personal Finance

Severity is a little harder, because it's subjective, and each person will have a different opinion.

Table 4: Risk Severity shows my opinion about the severity based on the time and cost of repairing my home, but you should adjust the figures for your circumstances.

I think if the repairs take less than a month, and cost less than $1,000, the severity is Slight. But if it takes more than 12 months, or costs more than $20,000, the severity is Tragic.

	Slight (<3%)	Minor (10%)	Fair (20%)	Major (33%)	Tragic (>33%)
Time	<1 month	1 – 2 months	3 – 6 months	7 – 12 months	>12 months
Cost	<$999	$1,00 - $4,499	$5,000 - $9,999	$10,000 - $19,999	>$20,000

Table 4: Risk Severity

Your Slight is the time and cost you're prepared to pay for an event. You might find it easier to start with the worst case and work back to more manageable territory.

You can also add additional rows for effects like injuries, family relationships, or lost income depending on your Virtues, Goals and consequences.

Back to our families:
- The Smiths are likely to have only a portion of the building damaged. Depending on the season, they could make the house safe themselves while they

wait for a builder to make proper repairs. Their scenario is Fair.
- If the Butcher's building is damaged by a falling tree, they could be denied access for months, and potentially forced to pay their mortgage and rent somewhere to live at the same time which would be Tragic!

Prioritise Your Risks

Next, remembering a risk is an event with a cause and effects, we need to rank them in the order they need to be managed.

Table 5: Risk Rating shows the likelihood in rows, and the severity in the columns, the cell where the intersect gives you the overall risk rating.

	Slight	Minor	Fair	Major	Tragic
Bound to	High	High	Severe	Severe	Severe
Likely	Fair	High	High	Severe	Severe
Possible	Low	Fair	High	Severe	Severe
Unlikely	Low	Low	Fair	High	Severe
Rare	Low	Low	Fair	High	High

Table 5: Risk Rating

For our families:
- The Smiths are Possible by Fair which is High risk.
- The Butchers are Rare by Tragic is also a High risk.

Manage the Risks

Having identified and prioritised your risks, the next step is to manage them.

Depending on your causes, you might find it's not feasible or possible to manage the Low or Fair risks, but both High and Severe ratings should be dealt with.

Both the Smiths and Butchers should manage the risk of a tree falling on their home. There are four main ways to do that:

- **Avoidance:** choose to withdraw from the risk situation. In this instance, the Butchers have chosen not to live in a forested area, but the Smiths will not.
- **Reduction:** reduce the probability or the impact. For example, remove trees near the house, or find and install some sort of device that would allow a tree to fall but prevent it reaching the house. Though it might not look pretty and will probably be expensive.
- **Retention:** accept the risk, particularly when there's little that you can do about it. This will work for the Butchers as we've already decided that a tree falling on their home is probably not going to be a problem. But, they should consider developing a contingency plan to deal with it. This isn't a sensible option for the Smiths.
- **Transfer:** pass the risk or consequence on to someone/thing else. In the Butcher's case, the risk is passed onto their building management; they don't have to think about the damage to the building. However, the Smiths should transfer the consequences to an insurance company - if a tree falls on their house, the insurance company will pay for the repairs (hopefully).

You can apply as many of these techniques as you feel comfortable with, and in most cases, you would use a combination of the most appropriate and achievable for you.

They should satisfactorily minimise the risks within your time, cost and ability constraints.

And most importantly, they shouldn't make the situation worse!

Contingency Plans

A contingency plan is like a risk management plan, but instead of taking action before the event to minimise the outcome, you don't act until the event is about to happen.

It's like a fall-back plan, and consists of identified actions to take when it's apparent they're needed; like hanging storm shutters. Or the Smiths pre-screening builders. You don't spend any time or money until you have to.

This is how you'll deal with many of the risk events you rated as low or fair as well as your seasonal preparations for extreme weather-related events.

Recovery Plans

Sometimes, the results are so much worse than you expect. You see it all the time on the television news; one house left standing while the rest of the neighbourhood is decimated. If you're not the one left standing, you'll need a recovery plan.

A recovery plan is your way to get back to normal; what to do, how much to spend, and how long it'll take.

With a plan, you'll not only be prepared, but may uncover additional risks or change your opinion about your risk ratings.

For the families:
- The Smiths could pre-screen builders, stockpile tarpaulins and other quick fix materials, and ensure Toby is unable to escape the property.
- The Butcher's might move in with Ash's sister for a few weeks until they know what's happening, save a few thousand dollars (so they have money available for an immediate move), and stay in contact with their real estate agent friend. They may have to put Tiger and Shadow in their usual cattery.

Personal Risks to Consider Managing

You're your greatest asset, in particular, your income generation potential. Your greatest risk is losing that potential.

Risk Event: You Are Injured or Become Ill

There's little in the way of happiness to be had without good health to enjoy it.

Here are some suggestions to manage your health risks.

- **Avoidance:** Choose to avoid risky activities and areas.

    Be aware of your surroundings, and if you're attacked, don't overestimate your hand to hand combat abilities - hand over your wallet and jewellery to avoid enraging your attacker.

    Don't allow yourself to be taken to a second location.

    Don't develop unhealthy habits.

    Buy cars, houses, and household goods that are less likely to injure you.

- **Reduction:** Eat, sleep and exercise well to maintain good health (see Chapter 13: Maintaining Your Health).

    When you've no choice but to undertake risky activities, consider using safety equipment to help to prevent injury.

    If you're afraid of stalking or kidnapping, vary your routine. Carrying a weapon won't benefit you if you can't use it properly, and increases the likelihood that it'll be turned on your or your children if they're with you. Take personal defence classes, and commit to regular training so you don't forget it.

Additionally, schedule annual physical and dental health check-ups to ensure you get ahead of potential health problems.

- **Retention:** There'll always be some residual risk you have no choice but to retain.

  This generally comes in the form of total incapacitation on life support, with no hope of reclaiming the life you had (see Chapter 20: Estate Planning).

  If you're facing a year or more of treatment, you might find it useful to develop a Health Care Plan detailing your treatments and required care.

  Collect all the relevant information into one place so you can share it with medical professionals, other caregivers and respite or palliative care facilities.

  Draw on all the resources you need for support; when people offer to help, tell them what you need.

  Schedule time for the primary carer to take care of their mental and physical needs.
  - Decide whether you need to hire professional carers and how you'll pay for them.
  - How you'll cover the additional costs of parking, takeout meals and childcare.
  - Whether you can negotiate a change in working hours.
  - How you're going to manage your emotions and keep family members informed.
- **Transfer:** Steering a path through the health care system is a journey worthy of immortalisation in an epic poem like Homer's *Iliad*, and it starts with buying full coverage health insurance.

  You'll want the best treatment, as soon as possible, and that's not possible without adequate cover.

Once you have it, use it to access preventative screening for chronic health conditions and early diagnosis of serious conditions like cancer.
- **Recovery:** Consider Long-Term Disability Insurance cover to replace a proportion of your income should you have to stop work.

    It becomes more important as you age; at 40 you're three times more likely to be disabled than die. The likelihood and duration of incapacity increases as you get older.

    Assess any cover provided by your employer, retirement savings scheme, or as part of your other financial arrangements before you buy.

    It will come with a waiting period and an expiry somewhere around retirement age.

    Look for a policy that covers injury *and* illness, renews automatically without re-qualification, and provides a top-up payment if you get paid work.

    Pay close attention to the occupations covered; some cover only your current job, while others cover any. This is important because you'll need an income while you retrain and look for a different occupation if you can't take up yours again.

    Try to find a policy that provides cover even if your employment becomes insecure or unreliable.

Risk Event: You Die

This one is about taking care of the people you leave behind.
- **Avoidance:** Sorry, no avoiding death.
- **Reduction:** Reduce the risk of early death by taking care of your health and not making rash choices.
- **Retention:** you have no choice but to retain this one. You need to focus on a recovery plan for others.

- **Transfer:** You can't transfer the risk. You can transfer some costs, for example, with funeral insurance. However, it may be more cost effective to open a high-interest savings account for this.
- **Recovery:** The original purpose of life insurance was to take care of your family in the event you died leaving them destitute, so if you don't have dependents, you don't need it.

If you do have dependents, but there would be sufficient income to cover family expenses, then you probably don't *need* life insurance either, but depending on your virtues, you might *want* some.

If there won't be enough money, then you definitely do need it, and if you want to make sure your family will be adequately protected, you need to think in terms of the worst-case scenario.

In the worst-case, your family would need to replace your entire income. This is best settled as a lump sum that can be invested to generate an income while preserving the original payment.

It'll be expensive, so shop around and perhaps select a cheaper policy with a lower settlement figure.

If you can't afford to provide an income, get a fixed sum to pay off your debts.

As you grow older, you'll accrue more savings for your retirement and pay down debt, and will need less life insurance. Typically, by 65 your need will have passed and you could add the payments to your retirement plan instead.

The most logical form of life insurance is fixed term life insurance. As the likelihood of your death is low for most of the policy period, the premiums will be too.

Term insurance comes in a range of lengths, generally one to twenty years depending on your jurisdiction, and needs.

A whole of life policy has higher premiums based on the assumption that a payment will be made. It has a cash value that can be bought back, but it's never going to be anywhere near the amount you put in as the value will be eaten away by long-tail commissions.

Risk Event: You Enter Long-Term Residential Care

This is primarily a concern for those over 50, but younger people who suffer severe injuries may find themselves in a care facility if their needs are greater than can be managed at home.

- **Avoidance:** Sadly, the better you look after yourself as a young person, the more likely you'll need long-term care. Best avoidance tactic is to die young, though this isn't an appealing option either!
- **Reduction:** Eat, sleep and exercise well to maintain good health. Try not to contract any long-term degenerative or cognitive diseases.
- **Retention:** Changes in medical technology and family structure mean you'll probably have to retain this one.

    Frightening as it is, and no matter how irrelevant it seems, make time to look into the cost of nursing home care.

    See what the basic costs are, and the cost of additional extras. Think about where that money is going to come from.

    Talk to your parents about their plans - are they relying on you to provide or pay for their care? How can you take care of them while you're caring for your children? Will you need to move into a bigger home?

Where will the money come from for that? And in the end, who's going to take care of you?

The situation will be different by the time it's your turn, but at least you'll have an idea of what to expect.

- **Transfer:** You can't transfer the risk, but you can transfer the cost with long-term-care insurance.

It may not be available in your jurisdiction yet, but it's useful to consider the costs you'll incur when you need to enter care, or secure appropriate care at home.

You'll be responsible for some or all of the care costs, and will essentially be paying for two homes. Which will probably chew through your savings and investments quickly potentially leaving your partner at home with nothing.

Long-term-care insurance might seem like a huge waste of money that could be better invested elsewhere, but like all insurances, (e.g., car, house and contents), you always hope you'll never need it.

Sadly, you're more likely to need long-term-care insurance than any other kind.

In 2015, the United Nations World Population Prospects gave the average lifespan for men as 67 and 69 for women. Bearing in mind, that diet, disease, healthcare and warfare vary dramatically around the world, the range is 15 years either side!

Start thinking about coverage around age 60, for an average stay of 10 - 15 years. Like life insurance, consider the policies in the light of how much cover you can afford over the long-term - you could be paying it for 15 – 20 years before you make a claim.

Take into account your potential retirement income and government or other assistances you may be entitled to or eligible for.

- **Recovery:** This will cost more than you think it will. While you're planning for the cost of care, make separate provisions to ensure there's something left for the one staying at home.

    You might like to consider trusts and other protective instruments (see Chapter 20: Estate Planning).

Household Risks to Consider Managing

In terms of stuff, your home is generally the biggest asset you'll acquire. Not only will you invest a lot in its purchase and maintenance, but you' probably use it to guarantee other borrowings too.

Some insurers exclude people who aren't policy holders, so ensure policies are in the name of all home owners. And if you move the property into a trust, make sure you put the policy in the trust's name.

Risk Event: Your Home is Damaged

Damage comes from external events (e.g., weather, fire, or careless drivers) or internal events (e.g., faulty plumbing, electrics, or fixtures).

- **Avoidance:** You can minimise internal events through judicious purchasing, but external events are largely out of your control.
- **Reduction:** Regular maintenance and replacement of external features like roofing and use of appropriate storm fixtures.

    Careful selection, maintenance, and replacement of internal appliances and fixtures that may fail and cause damage.
- **Retention:** You'll carry some risk because there'll be a point where this is the most practical choice.

- **Transfer:** You can't transfer the risk, but you can transfer the cost with building insurance.

    The insurer will decide whether the building can be repaired or must be replaced, so choose full replacement value.
- **Recovery:** This might include the cost of living somewhere else while you wait for the insurance company to approve payment.

    Ensure your children know how to evacuate your home in an emergency, can recite your name, address and phone number, and won't go away with strangers.

    You could use a code word to identify people they don't know who you have sent to get them. Make sure they know the emergency procedures at their school.

Risk Event: Your Goods are Stolen

While this can be very traumatic, don't risk your personal safety to protect your belongings.

- **Avoidance:** Don't make a big show of new purchases; dispose of the packaging discreetly.
- **Reduction:** Install window and door locks, external lighting, or an alarm system. If you're in a remote area, consider motion detectors and security cameras.
- **Retention:** Theft is more of a risk in some areas than others, and some people have more stuff than others. You may not need to worry about theft.
- **Transfer:** You can't transfer the risk, but you can transfer the cost with contents insurance; the best kind will be replacement cover.

    You'll need your inventory and may need to purchase specific cover for valuable items like jewellery, antiques or art above a given value.

    Don't forget to insure your car!

- **Recovery:** A Purchasing Plan for the replacements.

Risk Event: Someone is Injured on Your Property

The worst effect could be someone suing you. And even if they don't win, your legal costs could be crippling.

- **Avoidance:** You might find the likelihood of this increases with your wealth or public profile, and as your children reach driving age.
- **Reduction:** Maintain your property in a safe state. Only hire licensed, insured, and supervised trades with good reputations.
- **Retention:** If you're a "regular" private citizen, with a well-maintained property, you may feel comfortable retaining this risk. However, should someone sue and win you could lose everything.
- **Transfer:** you can't transfer the risk, but you can transfer the cost with liability insurance.

    Liability insurance covers you for injury to a third party or damage to their property.

    It's commonly included in homeowner and car insurances so examine your existing coverage to see if it's sufficient or you need a top up policy.

    Additionally, consider insurances you might need, like workers compensation to cover people you employ directly to work in or on your property.

    Depending on your circumstances, you might need additional cover for discrimination or harassment. Or extra liability insurance for trades and contractors.

- **Recovery:** Hopefully you're making plans to recover your good reputation rather than selling your assets to pay the bills. But you might still need to sell up and move somewhere else.

Other Risks You Could Think About Managing

There are other less obvious risks to consider.

Risk Event: Your Identity or Reputation is Stolen

Having your identity stolen is an event that's almost impossible to recover from.

- **Avoidance:** Where possible, keep a low profile and be careful about the information you put "out there."
- **Reduction:** Protect your home computers; not just from viruses, but malware, spyware and hackers too.

    Use additional encryption or private networks to protect your information.

    Do not invite strangers into your home, put a lock on your mailbox, and buy a shredder for personal documentation.

    Consider having confidential mail such as bank statements and utility bills sent by secure email, or to a secure location such as a post office box.

    Keep your original valuable documents like wills, powers of attorney, passports and other financial and identity documents in a secure off-site location (e.g., bank security deposit box).

    Store electronic copies on an encrypted, password protected USB flash or thumb drive, and a second copy somewhere secure but easily accessible in case the originals are sealed on your death. (See Chapter 6: Record Keeping).

    Ensure all staff you employ are working legally and you're complying with your obligations as an employer. Do background checks, and look for risk indicators like police investigations and bad credit. If you hire through an agency that claims to do checks, ask to see them.

Apply your basic checks equally across all staff, though you may prefer deeper or additional checks on those performing more sensitive or intimate work if that's legal where you live.

- **Retention:** You'll carry some risk regardless, so monitor your bank accounts and credit cards for unexpected transactions.

    Know when to expect your bills so you'll notice if they don't arrive.

    If you start getting bills and calls you aren't expecting from debt collectors, be prepared to act immediately.

- **Transfer:** You may be able to transfer some of the risk by hiring a reputable security firm to review your building, personal and information security.

    Get the most comprehensive check you can, and follow the recommendations.

- **Recovery:** You need a recovery plan because the sooner you act, the less damage there'll be.

    Immediately call the relevant companies about fraudulent transactions and ask them to freeze or close your accounts. You may need to arrange a cash withdraw to tide you over.

    Notify the relevant law enforcement authorities.

    Contact the credit bureaus and ask them to put a hold on any further credit applications until the situation is resolved.

    Get a copy of your credit report and notify them in writing of transactions and accounts that aren't yours.

    You should also notify the companies that have opened fraudulent accounts in your name.

Risk Event: You or Your Child is Kidnapped

Kidnapping is a risk for all people, at home as well as abroad. It might be:
- "Express" kidnapping where you're forced to withdraw money from an ATM.
- "Traditional" kidnap for ransom.
- Politically motivated kidnapping (e.g., by a terrorist group).

In each of these cases, you risk physical harm and potentially death.
- **Avoidance:** Before you travel, check your relevant Government department's website to determine your level of risk.

    Note that if the threat assessment is high, you may not be able to obtain travel insurance.

    Register your travel arrangements with your embassy in the country you're travelling to. If you're travelling for work, ask to see their security assessment.

    Take advice about how to control your children's presence on social media and so on.

    Perhaps use a service that monitors usage for key terms or new people.

    Limit the information you release yourself.
- **Reduction:** Women in particular need to adopt some precautions, such as dressing modestly and not wearing a lot of jewellery.

    I know, you shouldn't *have* to worry about it, but you would be wise to at least think about it.

    Stay in hotels with good security and facilities so you don't have to leave to eat or access cash. Have the hotel arrange transport for you, or book it before you leave.

Don't tell strangers about your arrangements, and try to avoid speaking to men you don't know in restaurants and bars.

Do not have people working in your home when your children are there. Teach your children about stranger danger, and particularly, teach your teenage daughters to avoid dangerous places, be aware of their surroundings, and be careful about what they say. Make them watch the movie *Taken*. Or make it a marathon with *Taken 2* and *Taken 3* as well.

If your child wants to participate in a group trip overseas, review the security plan. You're looking for some sort of systematic risk assessment, with steps in place to manage the risks (like you're doing now).

This includes issues like transport, housing, adult supervision, medical treatment, law enforcement.

For children at particular risk, (e.g., high-profile), consider hiring a security firm to review the plan.

- **Retention:** You can't completely eliminate this risk, so have a regular check-in procedure, such as calling home at 8 pm every day.

  If the call doesn't come, you know what to do. (You may need to make it plain that if the call doesn't come they will be the subject of an international man hunt).

- **Transfer:** You may be able to transfer some recovery costs with travel or specialist insurance.

- **Recovery:** Create electronic identity kits containing recent photographs, copies of passports and identity papers, fingerprints and a detailed description.

  Keep it up to date and ready to distribute to the police services should the worst come to the worst.

Bonus Tip: Develop a Disaster Recovery Plan

We've talked a lot about risk management and how to recover from risk events.

You've probably noticed there's a lot of similarity in the suggestions I have made.

That's because most risk events follow a similar path with similar consequences; it doesn't really matter whether your house burns down, is carried away by a tornado, or washed away in a flood.

The steps you're going to take to recover will be the same, regardless of whether they are big or small events.

1. Designate an emergency contact person outside of your area.

    A good first point is the International Red Cross, which operates a service you can call to register that you're safe, and others can call in to see if you've registered (and are safe).

    They can also take messages, like heading to or meeting at a given location.

    If your mobile phone is still working, change your message to say that you're ok on this date, at this time, and in this location.

2. Make some basic preparations for independence, because you could be on your own for several weeks depending on your location.

    Ensure you have food, water and medical supplies for at least three days. Ideally, in waterproof containers in bags you can easily carry if you need to evacuate.

    You'll also need a battery-operated radio and spare batteries.

Do some research about your area and risks (e.g., wildlife, sunburn, water borne diseases) and pack an appropriate emergency kit.
3. Each person should have their own kit, plus a larger combined car kit, all packed and ready to go.
4. Teach your children basic survival skills. Prepare and rehearse an emergency plan including evacuations and communications.
5. Research fire/storm/flood safety, emergency first aid, and how to leverage your slight body weight for lifting and moving items and people.

You may also find it useful to develop worst case scenarios and disaster plans for financial setbacks (you lose everything).

For example, if like the Butchers, you lost your home, you'll:

- Leave some spare clothes in your sister's basement so you can maintain a sense of normality.
- Put a few thousand dollars in a separate emergency housing account for bond and first month's rent.
- Move into your sister's basement (you might want to check she's ok with that).
- Get a job at a burger joint to keep some money coming in.
- And so on.

Summary

Unfortunately, life can be hard.

Circumstances can and do go bad at a moment's notice.

Managing risk is about preparing to deal with, and recover from unplanned events

- Remember, this is about protecting your vision of the future.

- Think about what might go wrong.
- Think about how bad it might get.
- Think about how to reduce the likelihood and consequences.
- Think about how to recover.

CHAPTER 13

Handling Your Health

ONE OF THE FUNDAMENTALS OF a wealthy life is the good health to enjoy it – there's no point being the richest hospital patient or corpse in the graveyard!

I've had my share of health issues, and I can assure you that there's little fun to be had watching life pass you by because you're too ill to take active part in it.

Ultimately there's no avoiding death, but your lifestyle choices make a difference in the quality and length of your life.

The top five causes of death are all "preventable;" heart disease, stroke, cancer, lung diseases, diabetes and dementia.

You can manage these killer conditions by making good choices about eating, sleeping and moving.

Manage Risk

Given that your unspoken goal is probably a long, happy, and healthy life, it makes sense to take a risk management approach to your health (see Chapter 12: Managing Risk).

- **Avoid:** what health risks do you need to remove from your life? For example, smoking, drug taking or midnight drag racing.
- **Reduce:** what do you need to do to reduce the impact of the risks you've identified? For example, less sitting, less junk food or fewer night shifts.
- **Retain**: what health risks do you need to consider contingencies for? For example, allergies, sports injuries or a family history of cancer.
- **Transfer:** what risks or consequences can you pass onto others? For example, buying health insurance, taking part in relevant medical trials or funding medical research.

Many of the solutions you come up with will reduce more than one risk at the same time.

For example, choosing to walk for 30 minutes a day will help you lose weight, strengthen your heart and other muscles, lower blood sugar, ease joint pain, and boost immune function.

It will also make you happier, more energetic, and improve your thinking.

That's a relatively quick and easy way to give each of your top five killers a little attention at the same time.

For bonus benefit, do it before breakfast!

And as part of your control method, stay up to date with advances in medical research and technology relating to the conditions you have a predisposition for.

Eat

Try to keep your weight under control because excess weight makes you more likely to contract chronic health conditions and die (according to insurers).

And others may judge you.

Regular, daily bowel movements are important for good health. If the bowels are not evacuated digestive toxins can back up and poison the body; just like a blocked sewer, causing headaches and fatigue.

To avoid constipation, eat fibre-rich foods like fruit, vegetables, and cereals, limit meat intake and drink plenty of water.

The Mayo Clinic recommends 13 cups of fluid for men and 9 for women (not just water).

Some fruit and vegetables, (e.g., watermelon, tomatoes and spinach) contain a lot of water and these count towards your fluid intake.

You may need to drink more in hot weather, if you're exercising intensely, are ill, pregnant or breastfeeding. Or less if you're not.

Aim to keep your urine colourless or a pale yellow.

Minimise your sugar intake.

If you have a problem with skipping meals, snacking, or eating too much at the meals you do get, consider scheduling your meals. This also helps minimise snacking, ensures time to rest, and prevents eating before active work or when tense.

Sleep

Sleeping well, and waking refreshed helps your memory, cognition and mood.

The current recommended sleep duration for adults is 7 - 9 hours per night, (pregnant women may need more). Teens and older adults should aim for 8 - 10 hours.

Daily exercise and a balanced diet can improve your sleep. Additionally, make some changes in your bedroom to improve your sleep quality:

- Keep your windows open a crack for fresh air. This is especially important if your heating or cooling has not been serviced recently and may be tainting the air.
- Keep it dark and quiet.
- Keep it cool; set your climate control to 60 - 68°F (15.5 - 20°C).
- Use a comfortable mattress (replace at least once a decade) and supportive pillows (replace annually).
- Turn off your electronic devices, or better still, don't take them to bed with you.

Move

Exercise develops fitness, stamina and resilience. What many people assume is tiredness from overwork, is more often poor diet, dehydration, constipation, inadequate ventilation, lack of exercise and worry.

Brisk outdoor activity like tennis, golf or basketball generates energy, gets fresh air in your lungs, and makes you perspire (eliminating toxins, reducing your susceptibility to some illnesses, and reducing pimples).

It's also fun, a change of scene, and an excuse to interact with other people.

The current recommendations for movement are:
- 150 minutes of moderate (e.g., walking, swimming, gardening), or 75 minutes of vigorous activity (e.g., running or dancing), or a combination of the two per week, plus
- Strength training for all major muscle groups at least twice a week.

The Mayo Clinic recommends 30 minutes a day (210 per week), in combination with reduced time spent sitting. For weight loss and greater health benefits, increase exercise to 300 minutes or more per week.

Stand up tall and breathe deeply. Give your organs and blood room to move so that you can stay alert, and keep your feet and hands warm. This also improves digestion and menstrual cramping. Exercises that develop your core strength will help improve your posture.

And if you can get away for a week to a health retreat, so much the better!

Rest

All it takes is 10 - 20 minutes of meditation or relaxation each day to de-stress and drop your blood pressure.

Knowing how your mind and body feel in this relaxed meditative state also makes it easier for you to stop in the middle of a stressful situation to consciously recall and replicate the feeling of calm

The easiest form of meditation is "mindfulness". All you need to do is sit or lie quietly being aware of your breathing and the way your body feels.

That's a bit boring, and your mind will wander, so when you become aware of that, you just bring your awareness back to your breath and the way your body feels.

You may find it easier to dismiss thoughts if you can name them, for example, "thinking", "worrying", or "planning".

Some find it easier to watch them as if they were a news report or a movie and let the thoughts wash over them.

It's hard (and sometimes frustrating) to do this, so you'll probably need to start with a few minutes and work up.

You might feel comforted to know that it's not an easy progression; no matter how practiced you are, you'll have some days that are harder or easier than normal.

If you don't feel up to meditation just yet, you can teach yourself how to relax instead.

Lie comfortably, take a few deep breaths and let your body go limp. If you're a bit tense, you may have to tell each part of your body to relax and let go. If you're not sure what relaxed feels like you might find it helpful to tense each part before you relax it.

You can do these practices at a time of day that suits your daily routine:
- In the morning to prepare to meet a busy or stressful day from a place of calm.
- In the early afternoon before the evening business of cooking, picking up kids and so on gets started.
- In the evening to let go of the pressures of the day and prepare for a good night's sleep

Friends

Life with friends is better than life without.

Aside from staving off loneliness, they help celebrate the good times and support you through the bad.

You're more likely to succeed in any health goal if you do it with friends.

Sometimes they'll even tell you your bum *does* look big in that dress, and this one is so much better!

Old friends can help you stay in touch with the person you were and hoped to become. Diverse friends expose you to different ways of thinking. New friends can inspire and motivate you to try new things.

But friendship is a choice. You have to choose to make time to maintain your friendships. It can also feel like a risk, because you have to put yourself out there.

Take a chance, and strengthen your friendships.

Learn

Many people focus narrowly on developing their careers during their downtime.

Housekeepers tend to spend theirs "talking shop" because they can't easily separate their work and leisure (it happens in the same place).

Regardless of who you are and what work you do, become a more interesting person by engaging in wider societal concerns; read books and newspapers, join clubs, participate in group sports, or pursue hobbies. Develop a philosophy of life.

Of course, to do this, you need to organise your home and work time to get the most important tasks done and stop worrying about the minor.

Or outsource the work you struggle with to others who enjoy it and can do it better than you.

Plan your leisure time to pursue your goals:
- Cultivate your virtues through involvement in your local community or active volunteer work.
- Deepen your relationship with your partner through shared experiences.
- Grow your relationships with your children by visiting museums, galleries, zoos and the like.

Manage Stress

The previous sections will go some way to managing your stress, but it's also useful to know what activities and which people stress you out so that you can take preventative action.

To help with this, you need to understand the difference between what you can control and what you can't.

For example, you can't control how long the bus trip to work takes, but you can choose to catch an earlier bus so you don't have to stress about being late.

Additionally, get to know how different kinds of schedule affect you, and plan routines that help you maintain the level of predictability you need.

Prepare for your peak workloads, and spread the load more evenly where you can. Try to balance your heavy work with light, and your sitting with standing too.

Set up your workspace so you can work comfortably and efficiently. Buy and use appliances, tools and fixtures that are the correct size for your body, and save effort rather than requiring more.

Schedule time with friends; share your thoughts and feelings with people who care about you. Listen to their problems too, sometimes knowing that their lives aren't perfect can help you cope with your own better.

Consider keeping a journal to write and discuss your thoughts and feelings about what's going on around you. Journalling is also useful for helping you work out solutions to problems and what to do next.

If you are experiencing intense stress that interferes with your enjoyment seek professional help.

Summary

Handling your health is one of the best ways to improve your wealth over the long-term.

- Identify and manage health risks.
- Eat, sleep and move to improve health.
- Develop your mind.
- Grow your friendships.
- Manage your stress.

CHAPTER 14

Owning a Business

THE WORLD IS STILL A place where women's pay and conditions are unequal to men's. If you're a well-educated woman, chances are you've already experienced this yourself.

You've probably learned some good business skills you could put to use developing your own business.

Take it from me, running your own business is quite frankly terrifying and exhilarating by turns, but it may be the only way you can redress some of the inequality in the business sphere.

Your workplace is as flexible as you need it to be, and your income potential may be greater than as an employee.

But while your business gives you working flexibility, it's the kind of flexibility that has you in your pyjamas at the kitchen counter at 3 am, not the kind where you're having coffee and cake with the other Mums at 11 am.

Having said that, if you want to go into business, you need something to sell, and it has to be something that people are willing to pay money for.

- A product, for example, a pair of Emily Baker's chandelier earrings, is a physical object that can be counted and measured.

  Yours might be a new version of an existing product or a new thing that's quicker, cheaper, or smaller.

  Product businesses are often expensive to run due to manufacturing costs, but they are scalable and offer the opportunity for healthy profit margins.

- A service provides an intangible result based on the provider's skill or knowledge, for example, physical training or dressmaking.

  Service businesses are generally inexpensive to run, but unless you take on employees, your ability to generate income is limited by the amount of time you have available.

Some services can scale into products like books or clothing lines.

You also need to decide whether your business will be primarily offline, based at a physical location your customers can visit, or online where all sales take place electronically.

- Offline businesses benefit from local visibility and the implication of professionalism and trustworthiness.

    Passing traffic increases business, and your customers can see and touch your products which may increase sales and reduce the cost of returns.

    However physical premises can be expensive to set up and maintain, you must watch your customers to reduce theft, and you can only sell when you're open.

- Online businesses are inexpensive and easy to set up (by comparison with an offline business).

    Your website is always open for business, and you have the potential for global rather than local sales, though this also increases your competition.

    It can be both easier and harder, as well as cheaper or more expensive attracting customers depending on your website and marketing knowledge.

- Hybrid business offers the best and worst of both.

    Potentially, not having some kind of online presence can limit your business growth as many people's first search is via the internet.

    You could start with a blog, and make additional income through endorsements or sponsorships.

    If you approach the right audience with the right topic at the right time, you can leverage them to build a successful business, but remember a blog is not a business unless it makes money.

The majority of new businesses fail within the first year, so give yourself the best possible chance and do some research before you commit your time and money to setting one up.

Will people buy your product/service? How much will they pay? How much will it cost for you to make? And so on.

Contact your local Small Business Department for advice on the tax and legal requirements in your jurisdiction, and join small business forums and groups for peer advice and support.

Businesses come in different types of formal and informal structures. This includes sole traders, partnerships with people, trusts, joint ventures and companies. Each of these has its own benefits and disadvantages.

It's a good idea to seek independent advice about the legal and accounting issues that go with each.

Plus, the related tax, income, deductions, retirement savings, banking, borrowings, payroll, insurances, and business record keeping issues as well.

Transitioning from Employment

If setting up your own business is part of your vision for the future, you have the opportunity to plan your transition from employed to self-employed.

That might mean setting up a "side business" you can work on outside of your hours of employment, gradually cutting them back as your business generates more work (and hopefully income).

Or cutting your living costs as much as possible so you can save a year or so of expenses to fall back on if the business doesn't grow as quickly as you hoped.

Running the Business

A lot of people (e.g., accountants, other business owners, and small business advisers) will tell you that it may take several years before a business turns a profit.

They'll tell you to set a budget, then try to sell a lot of products or services to cover your costs. And if you can't do that, take out a loan or credit card to keep the business going.

And this generally works well for larger, well established businesses turning over a cool million or two with employees pulling the load.

But if you're just starting out, struggling to make it on your own, with everything to lose? Well, not so much.

You've just read a few chapters advising you to look at what you've got coming in before working out how much you can spend. And there's no reason why you can't use more or less the same approach in business.

After all, bookeeping came about as a business tool way before before easy credit did.

No matter what some people say, a business that consistently spends more than it makes is headed for bankruptcy, taking its owners and everything they own with it.

Start by developing your business vision, mission and virtues. Then think about what you'd like to achieve and set some business goals.

Working In v Working On the Business

Running an owner operator small business involves two different kinds of time or tasks.
- **Working In:** doing the principal income generating work of the business; being, or making the product.

- **Working On:** the non-income producing executive functions like planning, professional development, managing the finances, and marketing the business.

All business are different, but estimates I've seen for working on the business range 20% – 40% of available time.

You'll need to experiment a bit, and where possible, develop systems and automations to prevent it spiralling out of control.

After a point, you'll have enough income to start hiring or outsourcing the finance and marketing aspects of running the business, but for best results, do the planning yourself, and keep developing your knowledge and skills.

Calculating Income

For the first couple of years at least, you'll have absolutely no idea how much money you're going to make. And it'll take you some time to understand what the seasonal flow will be. For example, do you sell well at Christmas, or is Valentines your peak season?

One place to start is by working out what you want your income to be, then add income taxes to the top for a total. Plus, if your business pays taxes too, add them in as well.

If you're planning a service business, you'll use your total income figure to calculate the selling price of your time. Don't forget to take your 40% executive time into cnsideration in your calculations.

In a product business, you'd calculate the cost of a single unit, and then how many you need to sell to cover the costs.

Bear in mind, that at least initially, there's not much point setting income goals you have little chance of meeting.

It's very easy to set a target of x hours or units, but each has a cost in time and money that needs to be controlled. And you're unlikely to sell much until you can attract buyers.

Minimising Costs

While you may not know what your income will be, you'll have some idea what your costs are going to be:
- If you're running a food business, you'll know what the cost of your ingredients are.
- If you're manufacturing, you'll have quotes for the manufacture and freight components.
- If you're selling your time, the cost of your phone, transport, paper and pens/electronic tablets and so on.

Just as in your personal expenses, it's very easy to buy what you *want*, rather than focusing on what you *need*.

Except when it comes to business, more of those wants can be considered needs.

For example, a top of the line phone with the right apps can be your inbox, calendar, document manager, records manager, finance manager, project manager, social media scheduler, marketing campaign manager, task manager, idea manager and payment gateway as well as your phone.

All of which potentially streamline your business and reduce the size and weight of your briefcase!

Making a Profit

Profit is essentially the income left over when you've paid your expenses. If you keep your expenses low, your profit will be higher.

Financing the Business

Businesses have two kinds of money needs:
- **Operating Expenses:** the day-to-day costs of running a business.
- **Capital Expenses:** once off cost of investing in the business; generally buying or upgrading assets.

Generally, operating expenses are covered by the income a business generates by selling its products or services. (And this is also where you cut costs if you need to).

But now and again, a business will need a larger sum for expenses like new equipment, setting up a new stock line, or developing new products.

Where possible, pay for capital expenses with your cash savings, at the time of purchase.

Avoid borrowing money for your business for as long as you can, because as I mentioned, it's likely your business will fail within the first year.

You may be eligible for grants or access to low-interest loan schemes, so contact your Small Business Department to see what's available.

Try not to draw on your retirement savings (see Chapter 11: Borrowing Money), because it may take several years for the business to cover your living expenses let alone top up your retirement savings.

If the time comes to borrow, carefully weigh up the pros and cons of the source:

- Friends or family – your lack of success and inability to repay the loan may undermine your relationships.
- Relying on your partner's income while you get established has similar problems.
- With an unproven business, your lender may want your home as security, which means you may lose it.
- For venture capital or similar investment arrangements, read the fine print because you could find yourself outvoted by your investors and forced in a direction you don't want your business to go. Or you could lose ownership of your business, and potentially your assets too.

Transitioning Out of Business

Assuming you make a success of your business, at some point, you'll want to get out of it as much, if not more than you wanted to get into it.

At that point, you'll need to develop a transition plan in consultation with your management team for selling it (to your management team, or a third party), transfer ownership to your children, or just close it down.

A staged transition is always the smoothest, and you'll need expert help for that.

Allow around five years to build a team of expert lawyers, accountants and business brokers with appropriate business, tax, estate and trusts knowledge and experience and get the appropriate changes in place.

The long transition time also gives you time to divest your emotional attachment and let go.

Other issues to consider include:

- Getting a professional valuation, so you know what you're working with.
- Review your partnership agreement for limitations on the sale or transfer of the business. Must you sell to your partners or can you sell to whoever you want?
- Can the business survive without you or is it about what you personally offer to your customers? Can you sell your branding or customer list?
- Your transition plan needs to take account of the business's liquidity. It might have significant assets and a high book value, but not be generating much income. And its debt is probably secured by your personal assets. What do you need to do to get your share out?

- If you're in a family business and want to pass it to your children, consider involving them from childhood (though this doesn't guarantee they will want the business as adults).

  Encourage them to achieve a suitable education and a Master of Business Administration. Insist they work in other businesses first so they're exposed to different ideas and processes that might benefit your business.

  This also gives them credibility and a demonstration of adequacy when they enter senior positions within the business.

  Make them work in similar conditions to their peers of the same age and rank, and earn the respect of their staff and managers.

  Ensure your senior staff are comfortable with the succession and include a changeover period of several years while you remain in an advisory capacity.
- If your kids don't want it, but you'd like it to stay in the family, can you sell it to another branch?
- Offer your management team a structured buyout; as a lump sum or instalments over time. (Your accountant can advise which course is best for you).

  If this is your preferred option, you need to start planning this well in advance to ensure they are ready when you are.
- If you're aiming at a third-party buyer, sell at the high shoulder point of the cycle when your buyers will make money rather than risking a sudden downturn that might take them a decade to recover. Aim for a cash sale rather than payment in stock.

Remember that your business, like your home, has an objective market value that's different to your subjective interpretation of the time and effort you've invested in it.

A sensible purchaser will look at what it costs to run compared to the income it brings. They'll consider the age and condition of its assets, and what they need to spend to upgrade. Their business goals and attitudes won't be the same as yours.

Summary

Running a business is terrifying and exhilarating. You can be successful by:

- Developing business vision, mission, virtues and goals.
- Working on as well as in your business.
- Minimising costs.
- Minimising loans/finance.
- Staying objective.

CHAPTER 15

Buying Property

WE TOUCHED ON THIS VERY lightly when we talked about Spending Plans, but I wanted to go a little deeper.

For the most part, I'll be talking about buying your future home, but I'm calling it "property" to try and keep the conversation on more of an objective business level than a subjective personal level.

The idea of buying property could be the trigger that starts you seriously managing your wealth.

It's a tax-effective investment, you can decorate it however you want, and you have that undefinable happy glow of home ownership.

And providing you keep your repayments up, you're not at the mercy of the changing whims or fortunes of property owners or managers.

On the other hand, houses cost a lot, and your mortgage repayments might be so massive that they prevent you from living a happy life.

The purchase and loan set up costs, taxes, duties, levies and other charges could be an additional significant burden - 10% or more of the purchase price depending on where you live.

Then there are the ongoing costs of maintenance, land taxes and levies as well.

But if you can afford a mortgage at two or three percentage points above what's currently on offer (as a contingency - see Chapter 12: Managing Risk), and are prepared to diligently pay it off for a significant part of your life then it's worth considering further.

Types of Property

Property comes in three major types:
- **Vacant Land:** has not been developed. On a personal level, it's usually bought in small lots to build houses

on. It also comes in larger acreages for agriculture or further commercial development, neither of which are within the scope of this book.

You could buy land as an investment, but there are ongoing costs of land ownership, and its value will not increase as quickly or substantially as developed land.

I recommend you don't buy vacant land unless you plan to build on it in the short-medium term.

- **Residential:** houses, apartments and so on for people to live in. Sometimes for yourself, sometimes as an investment to rent out to others.

    Investment properties could include short-term holiday lets or long-term rentals.
- **Commercial:** while commercial property can be vacant land, it's more often sold developed. Developments include offices, shops, and industrial units.

If you have a successful business, it may be worth buying commercial property for it, but as this book is about personal finance, I'm just going to tell you to seek professional advice.

Types of Property Ownership

There are several forms of property ownership. Depending on your jurisdiction they may have slightly different names and legal definitions so check for the detail where you live.

- **Sole Ownership:** you, as an individual, own the whole property. When you die, the property goes to the beneficiary you name in your will.
- **Joint Tenancy:** two or more people own equal shares.

    What happens when one of the shareholders dies depends on your location, the relationships between the shareholders and what's written on the Title (which comes from the contract of sale).

At one end of the spectrum, the share may be divided among the surviving shareholders. At the other end, the entire property may form part of the deceased estate and have to go through Probate.

If you're considering this type of ownership, take advice about how best to structure the contract and title deeds.

- **Tenants in Common:** two or more people own the property in stipulated percentage shares. They are free to sell or name beneficiaries for their share.

  Generally, an individual owner has no control over how the others disburse their share, and this can be difficult without a shared vision for the property.

  Consider taking advice on your options before entering into this kind of ownership arrangement.

- **Community Property:** Property bought by a married couple, belongs to a separate entity called the "Community of the Marriage", and each spouse owns an equal share of the Community.

  In some jurisdictions, it operates a little like Tenants in Common and in others like a trust, but either way, it gets *really* complicated where couples separate and don't divorce, or do divorce and remarry.

  If you're in this situation, get advice, and make sure that you include a review of your community property arrangements in your Annual Review.

Buying Residential Property

While you might assume that buying a home is just a natural part of growing up, you don't have to buy at a certain age or stage of life.

In fact, you don't *have* to buy at all depending on your vision and virtues.

But it's worth considering because property can generate income, provide a retirement residence, and depending what and where you buy, reduce your holiday costs.

When you're considering purchasing property, you need to screw your business head on firmly, and dispassionately weigh its merits as an investment vehicle before you start thinking about what it might be like to live in.

Life is unpredictable, and you never know when you might need to pack up and move because your job relocates, you get a better offer or want to cut your costs by moving to a less expensive home.

According to the 2010 US Census, Americans move 11.7 times during their lifetimes, and I would wager other Western countries aren't far behind. If you buy and sell a property each time, that's a lot of fees and taxes.

Additionally, you could lose money on a sale while paying an inflated price for your next purchase. It's financially sensible to at least consider renting out your home while you're away and renting something at your destination.

With that in mind, look for the best possible property in the best possible neighbourhood you can afford, as this gives you more options than a beautiful home that bankrupts you.

Think carefully about the location, condition and rental yield before you buy.

Short-term holiday lets provide higher rent than long-term rentals, but may be vacant for a larger proportion of the year.

Think about what people look for in their holiday properties and prioritise those features. For example, proximity to local attractions will be more important than green credentials.

In terms of risk management, a holiday rental that can also be let year-round as a home, will not only deliver income but maximise your sales yield as well.

If you choose an excellent location, the capital appreciation will cover your costs if the rental income does not.

If the property goes for rent, engage a respected firm of property managers with a good reputation to manage and maintain the property and maximise its yield. It's worth paying a little extra to ensure your property is well cared for.

Create a strong team of people to take care of your interests and the property; cleaners, gardeners, tradesmen, insurance brokers, tax agents and so on.

If your first property does well, you could consider buying another a few years down the track.

Bear in mind you'll want to minimise vacant time, so shop around for insurances and read the fine print to ensure coverage for local risks such as floods or storms.

And if you buy a holiday let, don't forget to book your stay ahead of time, or you might miss out!

Saving a Deposit

I hope you have a vivid vision because saving your deposit is going to be hard work. You'll need something like 10% - 20% of the purchase price depending on your location and lender.

I've added a sample savings plan at Appendix D.

Having said that, this discipline will also be good practice for managing your living costs when you move in.

As well as the balance of your savings accounts, your lender will be using your deposit history as an indicator of your ability to service the debt so keep them regular.

And for your own peace of mind, make them at least the mortgage repayment (+3%) minus your rent because you may end up having to find this amount every month.

If you can't consistently save that amount, you should start looking for less expensive properties you can comfortably pay for. It'll break your heart if you have to sell your home after you have emotionally invested in it.

You could take a second job to bump up your savings, but do you really want to live like that?

Look for other options in the organisation you work for, like higher paid jobs. You could also ask your family for help, but as I mentioned in Chapter 11: Borrowing Money, loans from friends or relatives can damage relationships.

Getting a Mortgage

It's a lot easier to obtain finance than it once was. My first mortgage application was rejected, and I worked for the bank! I had to wait and save more before trying twice more.

Your lender is more likely to fall over themselves to sell you a mortgage and associated products like credit cards and insurances.

That's because they're one of those businesses that make money off you - they're not a community service.

Pick your lender carefully. Compare the interest rates and fees they are charging. They may offer "free" benefits, but that just means the cost of them has already been factored into the offer and is not priced separately.

And if you're not going to use those benefits, it's not worth having them anyway.

You'll have a selection of loans ranging from fully variable (interest rates go up and down according to market forces) to fully fixed (the rate doesn't change for a period of time).

Fixed is good for predictability but you risk the rates going down. Variable is better when the interest rates go down, but they go up too.

Some lenders offer proportional loans where some is fixed and the rest variable. You have to choose the best according to your circumstances.

If you want a happy life free of mortgage stress, don't borrow more than you can afford to repay at that additional 3% margin.

Summary

Buying property (your future home) is a big step. It will require a significant investment of time and money, but will increase your Net Worth.

- Remember property ownership is not essential to a happy life.
- Think of property as an investment before thinking of it as a home.
- Consider taking advice about the best kind of ownership for you.
- Save as big a deposit as you can to reduce your costs later.
- Choose your lender carefully.

CHAPTER 16

Marriage

ONE OF THE MOST SIGNIFICANT DECISIONS you may make in your lifetime is to marry, whether that's a formal legal (as defined by law) arrangement or an informal one.

While we all like to think of marriage as the happily ever after fairy tale, they're more like a business partnership with constant ongoing negotiation and discussion.

And that's reasonable; for as long as the relationship lasts, and possibly for some time after, everything you do has some kind of impact on your partner.

Often, when love comes into the picture, we throw caution to the winds and expect the mythical ending regardless of all evidence to the contrary.

But, the fairy tale ends at "You may kiss the bride", and we don't see Cinderella cleaning toilets or washing socks and underpants.

Nor do we see Charming getting drunk at the pub because he didn't reach his sales targets and won't be getting the bonus they were counting on.

More than half of marriages end in divorce *because* of financial problems, so it's time to grow up and get serious.

You need to be able to talk as honestly and openly about money, as your sexual and emotional needs if not more.

Dating

If you've decided it's time to find a life partner, take a moment to consider the cost. Dates are expensive; new outfits, hair and beauty treatments – you've spent a couple of hundred before you leave the house. Then there's dinner, activities, and taxis.

And that's before you know whether being with this person makes you happy enough to consider emotionally investing in the relationship.

Finding a partner could cost you thousands of dollars, so if you're seriously looking for a long-term relationship, make provision for it in your Spending Plan.

Be specific as you calculate it; clothing, grooming, dating site fees, and babysitters as well as the cost of each date.

While you might imagine a tall, dark and handsome partner, with the same spiritual beliefs and life goals, look for someone with a similar vision of marriage and family life.

You don't need to talk about this on the second date, but if you develop some screening criteria, it will cut the time and cost of your search.

Issues to consider include who'll go out to work and who'll stay home to raise the kids. Or will you share and supplement with a nanny? Do you even want children?

If you're both honest, but can't negotiate an acceptable outcome, you can end it before either of you get in too deep.

That doesn't mean you can't still be friends, but at least you know your deep incompatibilities will prevent a long and happy marriage.

Avoiding Prince Humperdinck

Just to be sure, if you don't know who Prince Humperdinck is, he's the villain from the movie *Princess Bride*.

He wants to marry the heroine Buttercup, ostensibly to secure the royal line. But in "reality", has staged a kidnapping as an excuse to declare war on a neighbouring kingdom.

If you haven't worked it out, he has utterly no regard for Buttercup.

While you're searching for a partner, as well as considering their physical, spiritual and intellectual attractiveness, you need to assess their financial attractiveness too.

Put your business crown on, and look for behaviours you wouldn't accept from friends and colleagues. Be prepared to walk away - do not be tempted to sacrifice your financial independence for love.

Look for mismatches between what they say and do, and be especially wary of requests for money. If you're happy to support a less wealthy partner in the future, that's fine, but remember there's a cottage industry based on separating the dateless from everything they own.

I'm confident your vision isn't lovelorn and destitute.

Aside from con artists and gold diggers, you also need to beware of quarrelsome addicts who will feed their addictions with your money.

Gamblers are their own particular problem. It's perfectly legal, but it's an industry providing good returns to investors.

Social indicators include excessive interest in sports matches (because bets are on), but more concerning signs are wild mood swings, refusing to answer the phone, disappearing unexpectedly, and debt collectors at the door.

Gamblers also tend to deflect your interest in their affairs by undermining your confidence in your judgement, accusing you of spending too much money or being a bad partner.

If you choose to go ahead with a Humperdinck relationship, take some legal advice about drafting a prenuptial or cohabitation agreement.

At the very least you need to protect the assets you bring to the relationship and stipulate what happens to joint assets when the relationship ends.

Finding Prince Charming

Your best financial match is with someone whose financial style and priorities match yours.

If you're a time-poor professional, you could consider hiring a reputable professional matchmaker to pre-screen and weed out the Humperdincks and introduce you to like-minded partners with a similar status to you.

You'll have opinions about shared virtues and beliefs, and need to prioritise them according to your vision work:

- **Integrity:** Are they honest in their financial dealings? Do they pay their taxes in full and on time? Are their business expense claims legitimate? Is their credit card paid off or are charges being declined?

    If they seem dishonest in their dealings with others, it's likely they'll be dishonest with you too.

- **Realism:** Are they living within their income, or are they spending more than they earn?

    You could end up funding their lifestyle or living with an unhappy and unsatisfiable partner.

- **Negotiation Skills:** You might not have noticed it, but while dating, you're always negotiating about who will pay how much for what.

    This can be uncomfortable if one of you spends more than the other can afford to match. Or thinks they own you because they paid.

    You could be negotiating with them for the rest of your life, so pick someone you can work with.

- **Management:** Are they working and taking care of their expenses, or do they still live off their parents?

    If they manage their money, it's likely you'll be able to jointly manage your finances.

    Bonus points if they have a Spending Plan and are monitoring their spend.

- **Style:** Do you like their spending style? Are they too cheap, too profligate, or, just right? Will they sort coupons at the checkout or give mean tips at expensive hotels?

    If your financial styles are in conflict, you may end up struggling to open or close access to the joint finances.

When it Looks Like "It" Might Last

Generally, we're attracted to partners that balance us in all aspects of our lives, not just money.

And a marriage accidentally becomes a way that two people can test out their unconscious beliefs about gender, lifestyle and money.

For example, that women spend and men save, or that men do outside work and women inside. As your relationship deepens, you'll start testing out these assumptions and make new conscious agreements about your arrangements going forward

An important part of setting your baseline is providing full disclosure of your respective financials once you think the relationship might last the distance.

If it doesn't feel like the right time before, then certainly around the time you start talking about moving in together or getting married.

It starts by working out how to integrate your money beliefs and assumptions with theirs. Just like your other beliefs, these can reinforce the differences between you.

It's not very romantic, but if you want to be happy, you need to have at least one foot firmly planted on the ground.

In marriage, you may become responsible for your partner's debts (and they yours) so you both need to know what you are getting into.

As a minimum, you both need to share:
- **Income:** How much you earn, so you can decide how to split it.

  This will be difficult for business owners, or people who live on the proceeds of their investments, but you can take an average of the last few years.
- **Obligations:** For the young, this includes education debts, car loans, and credit cards.

  Older people may have alimony, child support, or mortgages. There may also be debts for health care, tax liabilities, and creditor agreements.

  Some will be mandatory (e.g., child support) and others discretionary (e.g., car loan).

  If your partner can't or won't produce a list, it suggests they're unaware of the extent of their debt, and possibly not meeting their repayments.

  If this is the case, you may like to take over that aspect of your financial arrangements.

  Or start dating again.
- **Credit Reports:** Credit reports record all applications for credit, as well as late payments, defaults, and any relevant legal judgements.

  As they're compiled by third party companies, they're generally independent and can't be manipulated, so they provide a good indicator of the creditworthiness of your partner.

  Occasionally, mistakes are made, or fraudulent activity takes place, so it's a good idea to access your record during your annual review so you can correct any errors.

  You can keep your record clean by making your payments on time, and not making too many credit applications.

- **Goals:** Your partner's goals of paying off their student loans or buying an investment property may require contributions from you.

    Some financial goals are also personal goals, like starting a business or buying into a partnership firm.

    Others, such as competing in seven marathons on seven continents in seven months require some intensive saving to cover their costs.

    Are these goals you can both get behind and make the sacrifices needed to bring them to fruition?

- **Handling Joint Finances:** How will you merge your financial lives?

    Do you/they need a prenuptial agreement?

    Are you comfortable opening joint accounts, or would you prefer to keep your banking separate and contribute proportionally?

    Consider including a plan to merge finances (with steps and date a year or two out) in your prenuptial.

    Don't rush to transfer your property into joint names, or agree to lease or finance agreements you can't support on your own.

If your partner doesn't want to discuss these issues with you before committing, it *is* a big deal and suggests they might be in an appalling financial situation.

Something involving illegal activities, false identities, and severe interpersonal problems looming close on your horizon.

You could keep dating on the hope they change their mind, but given your vision of a happily married future, you might be better to cut your losses and start looking for a more honest and open partner.

Choose the Prenuptial Agreement

At its most basic, the prenuptial details your individual assets and liabilities, and the property rights you will each have should the marriage end.

It won't be legally binding in all jurisdictions but like all formal contracts provides evidence of intent that judges consider carefully (see Chapter 18: Divorce).

While it sounds quite clinical to plan your divorce before you marry, statistics suggest your first marriage will end, if not within the first five years, then more likely within 10 - 15.

You might remarry, but more than half of second marriages also end in divorce.

Ex-wives often don't recover their financial situations, especially when they're the primary child care provider.

Prenups are not even a new thing; many cultures have a long history of arrangements being made to take care of wives at the death or divorce of their husbands.

Our reluctance to sign them, is just our insistence on fairy tale endings. Even when we don't really believe in them.

If nothing else, a prenuptial agreement gives you the opportunity to start taking care of your partner's needs before the marriage begins (which might be very useful if you have reason to believe your will may be contested).

You don't need to be fabulously wealthy to have one, you just need assets. But they're beneficial for those with:

- Investments.
- Valuable collections.
- A large potential inheritance, or
- Qualifications that represent excellent future earnings potential.

Additionally, those who are:

- Self-employed.

- The primary financial support for family members.

Without an agreement, you're at risk because you have no control over the outcome. Always assuming that lawyers don't get the bulk of it.

To start the process, take stock of your financial situation; list your assets, liabilities, income, expenses and credit report.

Think about the assets you might want to protect and retain after divorce, including intangibles like potential inheritances.

Then start talking with your partner, but be gentle because some won't understand the benefits or why you seemingly don't trust or love them.

Discussing your divorce *before* you marry is going to be awkward; choose your time and place wisely so you're both comfortable.

Be very matter of fact, use the same tone of voice you'd use to ask them to pass the salt at dinner.

Feel free to break it up into as many conversations as you need over time, but make sure you both understand you're talking about specifics, not making random plans for a potential future.

When you've nutted out the basics, it's time to get the lawyers involved, and you'll get the best results using different ones. The main issues you need to cover with them are:

- The different treatments of property and debts acquired before and after the wedding.
- The division of financial responsibilities during and after the marriage.
- What happens when one of you dies.
- Protecting business interests before, during, and after marriage.

You might also like to consider "sunset" clauses to provide end dates to some or all of your provisions.

A good lawyer will make other relevant suggestions based on your circumstances.

The Wedding

If, after all that, you make it to "I do," you still have to get through the Wedding Day.

While it's not possible to accurately generalise across the planet, the average marriage lasts around eight years, and regardless of who pays, the average wedding costs 25% - 75% of the couple's annual salary. Yes, both salaries combined.

If your wedding costs $35,000, that's $4,375 for each of the eight years of marriage. Which coincidentally, could pay for a pleasant generalised holiday each year instead.

If that's not bad enough, most weddings are financed with debt, and on average, take three to five years to pay off.

You could be divorcing shortly after you pay off the debt.

Alternatively, you could set a date far enough into the future that allows you to save some or all of the cost. And put the bonus income from your saving plan to good use.

Plus, you get the kind of discounts only achievable through early bookings, bulk purchasing, sales, and plenty of time to find and explore interesting new ideas.

Don't forget to get appropriate insurance cover.

Managing Your Wealth as a Couple

If you chose a partner whose financial style and goals match yours, you're in an excellent position to grow your wealth.

In Ancient times, households were essentially home businesses producing food, clothes, and other needs of existence.

They were managed by women because men were off at war, travelling the world to secure imports, or taking care of important government business.

In some cases, she managed the external business as well; negotiating sales, contracts, and so on. It took a brilliant woman to make it work.

More recently, Michel de Montaigne (1533 - 1592) expressed his satisfaction in having a wife he could rely on to take care of business while he got on with other duties. For him, her cleverness was far more important than her dowry.

Many businesses use a partnership structure, and this often includes senior partners who are responsible for generating income and junior partners who do the legwork.

If you look at your home in this light, you'll see both partners have an equal stake in its success. The income generator becomes the senior partner and the stay at home housekeeper the junior.

If you're the junior partner, you have the critical role.

Your housekeeping services would otherwise be outsourced, so while you may not be bringing in income, the tasks you undertake (e.g., cooking, cleaning, laundry, gardening, home maintenance, purchasing, nursing and childcare) would otherwise cost more than $100,000 each year.

As such, all income should be controlled by both partners, just as it would in business.

Both partners share the responsibility for saving and spending the entire income, because both share the risk, often equally regardless of who generates it.

This responsibility provides the motivation to keep your accounts up-to-date and accurate.

It is not for the senior partner to give the junior an allowance to cover their costs, but for the junior to draw against the business for legitimate expenses.

Allowances (also known as pocket money) are inappropriate for adults for many reasons.

One being that they prevent accurate planning and a business-like approach to spending.

Additionally, as they occur separately to the overall household financial goals, they lack context, and encourage excess and selfishness.

And force the recipient to beg for extra money when it's required.

It's more effective to work from a shared vision and virtues towards shared goals.

The junior partner needs to know *how much* can be spent, and the senior partner needs to know *where it's going*.

This ensures that purchasing decisions are in accord and business partners draw funds from the household accounts to buy goods in a "dignified" and adult way.

An agreed Spending Plan works towards shared goals (e.g., a rural property, or globe-trotting retirement), and eliminates the need to argue about money.

Both of you will only spend what is necessary until your goal is achieved.

You'll both be happy because you've agreed your end and the means you're using to get there; there's no room for confusion or misunderstandings.

But you still need to work together managing your finances.

It isn't fair to leave it for one to take all the responsibility. Your monthly reviews allow you to openly communicate about your financial situation, minimise confusion, and constrain your financial disagreements to a single meeting rather than ongoing guerrilla warfare.

Monitoring your investments together enables the benefit of both perspectives.

You'll be equally motivated to maximise your future income, and you can agree on divestment triggers such as x% loss where you sell regardless.

And of course, it's all up for grabs at your annual planning meeting.

You have the opportunity to debate what is and isn't working, adjust your vision, virtues and goals, and recast your spending and investment plans to match.

Summary

Joining your life to another creates a space for painful misunderstandings.

- Communicate openly and honestly about money.
- Manage finances together in support of shared goals.
- Don't start your marriage with a big wedding day debt.

CHAPTER 17

Children

LIKE MARRIAGE, CHILDREN ARE A significant life changing event that never quite turns out the way you expect.

Unlike marriage, you don't need to be in a relationship with another person to make it work.

It's a momentous decision with far-reaching implications, for yourself, your family and your children.

The Cost of Parenthood

We're in a time of flux over social beliefs about the roles of parents. There's some debate about whether choosing to stay home to care for children is selfish; depriving your country and economy of workers. Or whether you're depriving your kids of exposure to people with different skin colours and beliefs and therefore a well-rounded education.

These days married life doesn't require a wife to give up paid work to look after the children, though social stereotyping may mean that a working mother has to deal with criticism for not being a "proper" mum and a stay-at-home dad may be greeted with suspicion over his motives and capabilities.

It's unlikely you're in the financial position where both partners can stay home, though it might be possible for you to "job share" parenthood by both working part-time.

However, the most common solution is for the partner who earns the least to give up work.

This will lead to unpleasant feelings on both sides at different times, so it's important to keep the lines of communication open, talk through the issues, and reassess the non-financial costs of parenthood during your annual review.

It doesn't matter who supports whom, as long as you're both happy, or at the very least equally unhappy with the outcome.

If you aren't, you need to keep talking in the light of your shared vision (perhaps after a break) and start prioritising your virtues until you can come to an agreement.

Exactly the same as all your other important decisions.

Working Parenthood

Clearly working parenthood costs you money for care as well as time with your children.

You may miss out on many milestones; first step, first word, first ballet recital. You may face resentment at work when you arrive "late" or leave "early" to take care of family issues.

Or your relationships with your children may suffer when you use family time for work.

You might find you're exhausted all the time because you work all day and then come home and take care of the kids and house as well.

Stay at Home Parenthood

The stay at home parent will probably be responsible for the cleaning, cooking, and yard work as well as childcare.

As your children age there'll be school drop offs and pick-ups, homework supervision, and after school activities to co-ordinate.

It's a lot of work, and you may feel as though you're sacrificing the interests and activities that make you happy to get it all done.

However, the biggest risk for a stay at home parent is the lack of intellectual challenge that leads to the loss of identity, self-doubt and unhappiness.

Some will struggle with the awareness they're entirely dependent on their partner, and may feel that they're less entitled to spend income they don't provide to cover the cost associated with those activities.

Sacrificing activities that bring you happiness is not noble, nor does it make you a better parent (or person).

Continuing to pursue them makes you more pleasant to be around, and gives you something other than the kids to talk about.

And when your kids leave home, even if that seems a long way off, you won't miss them as much as if you had nothing else to occupy your time.

You also have the opportunity to start a home-based business, working around your children's needs. But the time you spend on your business comes at the cost of time with them, so think about your vision and virtues before you take the leap.

The Cost of Children

Children require your brains, brawn *and* wealth, but in return, they can be a personal *and* social good.

From their births to their deaths they cost money; clothes, furniture, food, doctors and care.

In 2015, the United States Department of Agriculture estimated that the cost of raising one child to 17 was $252,710 (inflation adjusted for 2019). This includes

> "budgetary components (housing, food, transportation, health care, and miscellaneous goods and services) and child-specific expenditure data for other components (clothing, child care, and education)".

Then there are college costs on top. That's a lot of additional spending, though of course you can't actually proportion food, operating and housing costs per person.

Getting Pregnant

Women are at their most fertile in their debt-laden twenties, and as access to paid and unpaid parental leave varies widely around the planet, you might choose to delay parenthood until you're on a sound financial footing.

However, this could lead to fertility issues and the increasing likelihood of birth defects.

Assisted reproduction through in vitro fertilisation (IVF) could cost more than $100,000 and does not guarantee a pregnancy. If you're in your thirties and want to keep your options open, consider freezing some eggs.

This costs around $15,000 and is probably not covered by your health insurance (except possibly if you are about to undergo cancer or other treatment that will render you infertile).

Freezing your eggs doesn't guarantee a pregnancy either, but at the current stage of technology, it's more likely to result in a viable embryo than IVF.

Before you commit yourself to parenthood, consider when you'll bear your children, and what will best meet their needs. Do you want to be 45 running around after a two-year-old? Sixty at your child's high school graduation?

If you reach an age where you decide not to proceed with a pregnancy, depending on your jurisdiction, you may be able to donate your eggs to someone who is infertile.

Or if not, you can destroy them, unlike an embryo that belongs jointly to your sperm donor.

Living Costs

Where you or your partner take time off work to care for your children, they will add 3 - 10% to your food, housing, clothing and operating costs, and this will most likely come from your provisions for a happy life.

The cost of an infant is unpredictable for the first couple of years, but after that, it's more about home efficiency and parental capability.

Two children don't cost twice as much as one; clothes and equipment bought for the first can be used by the second (and depending on the quality perhaps a third).

They will entertain themselves (leaving you to get on with your chores), and older children are inexpensive babysitters for the younger ones.

Additional children are not a compelling excuse to up-size your life and move into a bigger property.

As I mentioned in Chapter 3: Spending Plan, a bigger house increases your operating costs. And a bigger house in a "better" area may increase the cost of satisfying your children's wants as they try to keep up with their peers.

If you don't have a clear vision for the new property, it cannot provide the benefits you are seeking.

School Education

School tuition can cost $5,000 to $20,000 per year, plus uniforms, bags, books, school trips, musical instruments, sports gear and computer hardware.

University Education

In the 2014-15 school year, the average cost of tuition and fees at an American university was between $9,000 and $31,000.

At the time of publication, many other countries required a similar numerical commitment (i.e., in British pounds, Canadian, Australian or New Zealand dollars).

When the time comes, you may need to make compromises, but don't go into debt to buy your child's education.

You can send them to a cheaper school, apply for scholarships or tell them to get jobs.

But, just like your retirement savings, the sooner you start putting money away for their education, the more you will have when the time comes.

And just like all your other accounts, you need to do some research and find the best option for you and them for income and taxation.

If your children are accustomed to living well at home, they will expect the same (if not better) if they move away to study so you may be up for a substantial pocket money increase too!

Plus, housing, books, clothes, mobile phone, health insurance, vehicle maintenance costs, and the like on the top.

Even at that price, university education still increases your children's likelihood of more opportunities and higher wages, so make your desire for them to go to college clear, as well as your ability to pay for it.

Encourage them to get good grades and pursue activities that could lead to scholarships.

Suggest they attend University full-time after high school when it's easier to complete their course than later when they are working full-time and trying to study on the side (you can take that one from me too).

Teaching Your Children About Money

Your kids need to know about money because wealth management is an important life skill that provides the opportunity to pursue a lifestyle beyond the scope of minimum wage.

Even if you're relatively affluent as a family, your children are not, and more than their poorer peers they must learn to manage themselves and their money responsibly.

If only so that they don't blow your legacy.

Giving into your child's whims won't make them happy, productive, or self-sufficient in the longer term.

They need to learn the difference between their *needs* and *wants*, and how to delay immediate gratification for a long-term benefit.

While you may be able to afford what they want, they need to know that spending, saving and sharing are choices made in line with their virtues and priorities.

That might include a second-hand GMC, but not a brand-new BMW.

When they're young, play buying games to teach them about value.

As they get older, explain how advertising works, what credit cards, ATMs, insurances and mortgages do - show them how the world actually works.

Set an Example

Let your children see you engaged in work you enjoy, studying hard for future opportunities, or running a little business on the side.

Live within your Spending Plan and make responsible decisions that safeguard your future.

Include them in your wealth management cycle; planning, monitoring and controlling spending.

Explain your vision and virtues and let them see you using them to guide your choices.

This will be particularly useful for blended families to demonstrate all children are receiving equal consideration.

They'll understand your priorities and the sacrifices this may require, and they'll want to do their bit for a shared goal such as a vacation, property, or education.

Encourage Their Potential and Promote Their Strength

Encourage your kids to explore their interests and give them the opportunity to discover who they are.

Don't shut them down by telling them they're stupid or should focus on getting a proper job.

Twin studies suggest genetics are more important than their home situation, so let them dream big and develop their talents to the extent they want to.

Help them work out the realities of income and costs for their dream jobs, cars, or hobbies, but let them make up their own minds.

Teach the Importance of the Big Three

We all learn best by practising, so give your children pocket money, and the space to fail so they understand the consequences before it *really* matters.

Follow the lead of John D Rockefeller Jnr, and teach them to save (e.g., 20%) and share (20%) their pocket money as well as spend it. Ask them to keep an account book and review it with them.

Offer incentives (e.g., matching savings) for compliance and penalties (e.g., reducing their pocket money) for not.

Your children will enjoy watching their savings grow, feel the benefits of helping others, and develop the sound accounting and financial decision-making habits they'll need when they leave home.

Connect Your Children with Reality

If you're well-off and don't want to see your kids featured in tabloids with a string of drink driving convictions, another stint in a rehabilitation facility, or the complete inability to grow up and behave like a reasonable human you need to give them a solid foundation.

Teach them your family virtues, encourage them to get a good education and build a career that provides purpose or grows the family fortune.

If it's unlikely they'll "work", they should at the very least know how to read financial statements and manage the investments they'll be living off.

Your efforts to teach them the interpersonal skills they'll need to deal with funding requests and the professionals who manage their fortune will be appreciated.

Raise them to connect meaningfully with the world and other people rather than fritter away your gifts on lavish lifestyles and trophy partners.

Blended Families

Many modern marriages are between divorcées who bring children to form a blended family.

Before you enter into a second or later marriage, consider the impact on your children's emotional well-being as well as your finances; both sets of children are facing an even more significant change on top of a previous divorce that they may not have come to terms with.

A second marriage could bring obligations to three sets of children; those from your first marriage, your second marriage, and your second partner's children too.

Regardless of the formal arrangements you make, it's useful to work on the assumption that you'll be responsible for all of them at some point.

You and your new partner need to be very clear about how you are going to manage the family.

The Children's Well-being

The age of your kids will have the most impact.

Younger children bond more easily and deeply than older children who have left home. Young children may be sent to boarding school or older children primarily cared for by their birth parent.

Blending is easier for children when they can see they're all treated fairly in the new relationship. Either they all go to private school, or all go public. They all go to camp, or they all get summer jobs.

Will they all have their own room, share with blood relatives or step siblings?

Will their standard of living be lowered or raised?

Will they be ok with that?

The Financial Impact

You need to be even more vigilant examining your second partner's financials than your first because you need to consider the impact of their financial modelling on your children.

Similarly, a prenuptial is even more important than the first time around.

You must each also disclose your child support and alimony obligations.

How will you manage the costs of your combined household if most of one partner's income is committed to those obligations?

Will you allocate some of your income towards their obligations, divide costs proportionally according to the number of children, or equally?

If you merge your financial and parental responsibilities, who will be the primary carer?

Who covers which children's costs?

Who makes which decisions?

How will you teach your children about money?

Most people assume that when they die, their assets pass to their blood relatives, and if that is what you want you must make it clear in both your prenuptial and your will.

With three sets of children to consider, it may be helpful to set up a trust, so consider taking professional advice.

Careers in the Public Eye

Attractive or athletic children may end up with a successful life in the public eye, but the path to stardom can also lead to ruin for the whole family and must be managed well.

It'll require a lot of time in auditions or try-outs, performances or matches, and competitions. If you can't take care of this, you must hire someone who can.

If you handle it, consider the impact on the children you leave at home. If one child seems to be receiving too much money or time, there will be friction.

You also need to consider how you'll cope if the child is injured and needs care.

Enormous opportunities such as movies shot in international locations come at tremendous cost to schooling and family life as the child, and a parent or guardian must relocate for the duration.

Most childhood "careers" do not survive the transition to adulthood, so keep them focused on getting a good education.

Whether it survives long-term or not, involve your child in managing the business side as well.

Some will make more money from endorsements than their passion, so encourage them to attend and participate in meetings and choose their endorsements (according to their vision and virtues).

Consult your financial adviser and lawyer about how to protect their money through to age 25 or so while allowing their education expenses to be drawn down.

Sports

If your child's vision doesn't include superstar status, they won't be committed to making the sacrifices required to achieve it, such as long training sessions and camps, injuries, and time away from the family.

Or they might not be talented enough to make it big, or take a career killing injury, and need to be guided in another direction before too much time and money have been spent.

At some point, to protect their career, you'll have to take a step back and hand them over to the professionals. You'll need trainers, lawyers, and managers who have the time, knowledge and skills to get your child to the next level without offending the decision makers.

Acting and Modelling

There are a lot of child predators out there, so if you're approached by someone, take a business card and thoroughly research the company before you commit to anything.

You'll also need to monitor the child's mental well-being as being constantly judged by their appearance can be hurtful, and you have no control over how the rejections are delivered.

Additionally, your child may develop people pleasing behaviours in an attempt to gain approval and work. Or separation anxiety when having to enter a room alone to audition.

You may need to place limits on what and when they work, and you need to be prepared to pull your children out of work if the content is substantially different to what was initially proposed, for example, dealing with abuse scenarios.

You also need to buy the materials and equipment they require (e.g., headshots and classes including topics like respecting clients, mindset, and understanding photo shoots) and build a professional team who will protect them.

Their acting/modelling income probably won't cover their costs initially, and could take three to five years at around $3,000 per year before you know whether a longer-term career is realistic.

Be prepared to help them make difficult decisions.

Similar to sporting, a child that makes it big needs to be placed in the care of professional agents and managers to further develop their careers.

They'll have greater expenses, but be making bigger money, so there'll be enough left to require careful management until your child reaches their majority.

Furry Kids

There are many benefits to having a pet, but I am not going to go into them. You either are or are not a pet person.

You can pick up an inexpensive pet in good health at an animal shelter, but their behaviour will not be as predictable as a more expensive pure breed.

However, many pure breed animals come with the additional cost of inbred conditions.

Ordinary care (vaccinations, worming, and vet check-ups) can add up to $40,000 over a 14-year lifespan (not including critical care).

Advances in medical technology benefit pets as much as people, and along with their increased lifespans come increased medical costs due to serious illnesses like cancer.

You can buy health insurances for pets, but check the small print as the items you can claim for are generally quite limited, and you might be better to self-insure by opening a designated savings account for medical expenses.

Obedience training is a must for a responsible dog owner.

Not only will it prevent property damage (and possibly litigation), but it will also safeguard your pet's welfare if they come when called, or stay on command.

Consider making provisions for your pet should you die or become disabled during its lifetime. Ask someone you trust to take care of it should this happen.

Having named your pet's guardian, teach them how to take care of its needs. Consider investing the lifetime cost of your pet's care in a trust and name your guardian as the recipient for the pet's life.

For peace of mind, you might like to nominate an independent third-party trustee to manage the fund.

You could also make separate provision for any funds remaining after the pet's death.

Ensure all relevant parties know what the provisions are for the pet.

Taking care of it separately to your will ensures your wishes can be implemented quickly, and its well-being taken care of no matter how long it takes for your estate to settle.

Though, you might like to develop a contingency plan just in case.

Summary

Children are yours forever. If you teach them how to take care of their finances, they are less likely to be a drain on your retirement funds.

- Think carefully about who will be their primary carer, and ensure that person has the time and space to live a fulfilling life outside of that roll.

- Save for predictable costs like their education.
- If you marry two or more times, carefully consider your relationships with all the children, and treat them equally.
- If your child turns out to be good at sports or acting, take care of their needs but don't forget your other children.
- Make provisions to take care of your pets after you've gone.

CHAPTER 18

Divorce

WHILE WE ALL DREAM OF marriage and living happily ever after, there is a chance it won't last, and you need to be prepared for that.

Divorce isn't easy, but it can be dignified.

Pre-Divorce

Hopefully, you started your marriage with a prenuptial agreement (see Chapter 16: Marriage) that excluded your premarital and trust assets from the marriage.

If you gave your partner access to them, you have now lost control of them. You partner may not account for what they've done, and it may be lost to you forever.

And this is why you need to stay in touch with your family finances. When you're up to date with them, your partner has little opportunity to hide assets, though they can still be concealed in undervalued or business assets.

If you don't want to do the monthly review meetings (and you really should), at least review your annual tax return and check your credit reference file.

Keep your own copies of all the financial documents and make sure you understand them and their implications. Take independent advice if you need to.

Maintaining a separate bank and credit card account could be useful. They give you a little breathing space if your partner empties all your accounts before disappearing, divorcing, or dying. And they're also useful if you're the one that needs to disappear or divorce.

If you're being physically abused, keep records of dates and injuries, with photos if possible. Seek medical treatment as this provides independent corroborating evidence. Also note other intimidatory or bullying tactics that take a mental toll.

If possible, when the marriage starts to become problematic, make a postnuptial agreement. It's like a prenuptial but describes what will happen if the marriage ends instead of improving.

Once you know the marriage will not survive, give yourself some time to get your affairs in order.

If you haven't already, set up your accounts and start saving. Think about your new Vision, Mission and Virtues, then take some legal and financial advice, and get some counselling.

Generally, the laws that cover the dissolution of marriage are those of the place where you have resided for the six to twelve months prior.

There are variations on property, child custody and so on, so local advice is essential.

If you believe your partner may be hiding assets in their business, you could consider hiring a forensic accountant to review the records.

Make sure you understand the real value of your assets, including the taxes payable on liquidation.

Think deeply about whether you can afford to maintain your home without your partner's income; your lifestyle may change dramatically, but you could be better off with a smaller house and more money.

Initiating Divorce

Don't take advice from friends or relatives, regardless of how qualified they may be.

Be deeply suspicious of kind strangers (con artists) offering to help.

As an involved party, it's unlikely you will be able to negotiate your best outcome, so hire the best lawyer you can afford.

This is particularly important where children's interests need to be protected. Be prepared for short-term pain to ensure their long-term gain.

The time and manner of bringing up the subject of divorce can have a big impact on how hard the process is. Be sensitive to other events in your partner's life - don't tell them the day after they get made redundant.

Rehearse what you want to say, and try different ways of saying it. You can, of course, rely on your lawyer to do the talking, but you'll be paying them for that.

In any case, you'll have to speak calmly and authoritatively with your ex sooner or later, so you might as well start practising it now.

If you're unprepared for your partner asking for a divorce, and you haven't already, immediately open bank accounts so you can operate independently.

As time passes, it may be more difficult for both of you to behave rationally, so get your affairs and team in place as quickly as possible.

Avoid escalating the situation to all out warfare.

Keep your costs down by being reasonable about your demands and settling fairly as quickly as possible.

Post-Divorce

Alimony is a spousal support payment made by one partner to the lesser earning partner after a separation or divorce.

It is not a right, and the amount and duration are generally determined by the Court on the basis of need related to the marital lifestyle.

If you've been the breadwinner, don't be surprised if you become the one paying alimony

Child support is a payment made to the partner who will be the primary carer post-divorce.

It's separate to spousal support arrangements, and usually only covers essentials, not discretionary items like ballet lessons, school trips or new smartphones.

Try to negotiate agreement about how the extras can be paid for as part of the divorce settlement.

In terms of risk management, ensure a life insurance policy covering your payments is included in the settlement.

Where possible, make it a single premium policy so it won't lapse if the renewal isn't paid.

This is crucial if your partner remarries and has a second family. While we wish it were otherwise, the first family can be easily forgotten in the daily hassle of the second family.

Summary

Divorce is a messy and often traumatic transition from one stage of life to another.

- Stay future focused by developing new Vision, Mission and Virtues, and use them to navigate decisions as they come up.
- Make your children's welfare more important than your pride and pain.
- When times get tough, take a deep breath and walk away. Try again another day.

CHAPTER 19

Retirement

IN THE OLD DAYS, IT was unlikely you'd live long enough to retire - at best, you might expect a year or two past the end of your working life.

These days you could work for forty and live another forty as well. On top of that, women are likely to outlive their male partners by 5 – 10 years.

If you're physically well, you owe it to yourself to find something to occupy your mind.

And if you aren't well right now, consider that medical technology has already progressed to the point where you can grow a few of your cells into skin and veins, or use three-dimensionally printed organ frameworks for ears, oesophaguses and vaginas.

It might take a little longer, but it's not beyond the realms of possibility that in a couple of decades you may be able to grow new organs to replace worn out ones, and who knows how much longer you might live then!

There might be a mandated retirement age where you live, but you will probably continue to "work" in some fashion:

- As an unpaid volunteer for a cause you care about.
- For part-time income.
- For free, taking care of your grandchildren while your children go out to work.

Regardless of the work you prefer, you need to plan for it.

If you're a forward thinker, you have no reason to be afraid. By the time you retire, you'll understand your capabilities and have an excellent idea of what you want to do next.

As long as you have income, that can be anything you want; travelling, studying Medieval French Literature, or perfecting your watercolour painting.

Planning for Retirement

The basics you'll need for a happy retirement, are the same things you need right now; money, health (both physical and mental), and time.

While we've been talking about five-year visions, you also need to take a more speculative view of what your post-work life might look like.

I don't have a crystal ball (well I do actually, it's sodalite), and I can't predict the future, but I can imagine what it might look like.

> As the population ages, governments will try to limit their social welfare and health care liabilities, for example;
>
> - Raising minimum retirement ages rather than decreasing compulsory retirement.
>
> - Reducing payments and increasing barriers to accessing old age benefits.
>
> - Taking control of the pool of retirement savings.
>
> Employers will claim they can't afford to give pay rises let alone increase retirement contributions.
>
> Retirement funds will change the way they calculate benefit repayments, perhaps limiting access to your capital.
>
> There will be even greater advances in medical technology that mean our bodies could outlive our will to live. We may not have a safe and legal way to end our lives, and to prevent us illegally taking our own lives, death will only be permitted in medical facilities.

That could be a pretty grim, future.

It seems prudent to start thinking now about how you might independently fund your retirement.

How much money you need ultimately depends on what you want to spend it on (e.g., local or international travel), and to an extent that depends on having the level of health that will support those activities.

This isn't something other people can do for you, you have to work it out yourself and plan accordingly.

Connecting with Your Future Self

Part of the problem of planning for your retirement is that it's hard to emotionally connect with your future self.

This makes sacrificing your money now so they can live comfortably quite difficult - much harder than sacrificing for your children or your parents.

To fix this, you need to make future you a real, and emotionally important part of your current life.

One way to do this is to take a recent photo of yourself and age it to something like 70 or 80 when you'll need the money you might not be saving just yet.

Keep it with your family photos or on your desk where you can see it regularly, and your future self will become a face you are familiar with and who's worthy of some thought.

Or for a more shockingly realistic experience, hire a makeup artist to give you an ageing makeover and take a long hard look in a mirror.

If you don't want to go that far, start a letter conversation with an older version of you. This person knows exactly what's bothering you right now (they've already done what you're thinking about). Tell them what you're worried about, and ask for their advice.

Then write back what you think an older and wiser version of you might say in return.

If you find it hard to get started, try writing a letter to yourself at a time in the past when you were struggling.

Most people tend to think of themselves as fully developed psychologically, and expect to stay the same for the rest of their lives. So, try imagining yourself at 70 doing something you enjoy now.

If you enjoy a good long walk like the Butcher family, imagine doing that at 70. How do you need to take care of yourself physically to achieve that? How much money do you need to travel the world every other year for a walking holiday?

And of course, reconnect with your vision of the future by putting yourself right in the middle of your retirement. Are you living in a squat eating cat food from the can or strolling around a golf course at the peak of health?

Money

You need to take a long hard look at your finances; when can you retire comfortably?

How are you going to fund your retirement? How can you maximise your retirement savings?

The sooner you start, the longer you can spend travelling.

Depending on where you live, your retirement income will come from a combination of private savings, and employer-sponsored retirement savings within a legislated framework (e.g., the 401(k) in the US, occupational pension schemes in the UK, Registered Retirement Savings Plan in Canada or Superannuation in Australia and New Zealand).

- **Employer Sponsored Saving:** When your employer puts you into a plan, they contribute an amount separate to your income and offer you the opportunity to add pre-tax funds as well.

  They invest that money on your behalf, but as that's a lot of hard work they usually outsource it to an investment firm.

  Depending on your jurisdiction, when you change employer you can leave your retirement plan where it is, transfer to your new employer's plan, or instruct your employer to contribute to your existing plan.

To avoid duplicate fees, consolidate into a single plan that best meets your needs.

One of the advantages of these types of schemes is the legislation generally provides for tax-free or reduced tax savings.

There's usually a cut-off point where the tax-free benefit ceases, so get advice and take full advantage of the benefits in your jurisdiction.

The money you put in is important, but the tax you don't pay is more important - it enters your plan tax-free, *and* potentially reduces your regular tax payments (jurisdiction dependent).

These tax benefits make retirement savings plans the best places for your retirement savings when you don't have a lot to spare - a tiny bit each pay is barely noticeable.

- **Private Saving:** Private retirement saving could be additional retirement accounts or other investments.

    Most governments legislate maximum reduced or tax-free retirement contributions, so take this into account when you're choosing your investment vehicles.

    Educate yourself about how your system works.

    Self-employed people have the option of retirement savings plans designed with them in mind; they often fall under different legislative arrangements.

    You may also have to make provisions for the retirement savings of your employees. You should seek advice from a local qualified professional.

The key thing to note about retirement savings is that time is the most important ingredient. Savings accruing from age 20 will be larger than those starting at 45.

Not only is more money going in, but your returns are growing too - thanks to compound interest, dividend reinvestment and dollar cost averaging, the more you have, the more you earn.

Keep this in mind when you think about your current plans – your Paris vacation will cost earned interest as well as capital. Not that you *can't* take the trip, but once you spend that money, it and the potential benefits are gone.

When you're planning your trip, take your future into account as well; maybe postpone it, take a cheaper package, or make the most of it, so you remember it for a very long time (while you're living in that squat eating cat food).

You can't rely on a steady rate of return for the life of your investments, so you need to plan on a random basis, and a Monte Carlo simulation is good for that.

The simulation works by developing the best, worst and most likely scenarios and returning a probability of success.

Many financial institutions offer free online simulators so you can test the impact of different incomes and spending.

Your investment needs change as you approach retirement. You need to think about reducing your risk profile to preserve both your capital and income streams.

If your partner has been doing the bulk of investing (and you haven't been keeping up with it), start getting more involved. Make sure you understand the investment strategy and agree on the risk profile.

Discuss whether you should buy, increase, or decrease your life insurances. Consider diversifying your investments further, and examine all potential long and short-term income producing options.

Health

Start taking very special care of your body; eat well, get some exercise and make good sleep a priority.

Consider taking some counselling to heal and release old emotional wounds that might be holding you back.

Meet and mix with new people who support your new goals; like those seven marathons.

Remember that you might live to 100, so make it count.

Time

What you do with your time may not significantly change in the short-term, but your calendar will completely open up overnight. You need to consider what "work" you will fill your retirement days with.

Your life-long virtue of Independence might lead you to paid work as a house mother or caretaker where your room and board are included in your salary package.

Life as a charming host might become a retirement running a bed and breakfast where you're booked solid by friends and paying guests. And you may receive so many return invitations that you can stay away for the worst of the arthritis inducing cold winters.

You could help out your married child by buying a house with a self-contained apartment and invite them to take the main house. You can maintain your independent life while helping them, and they can help you too.

If you have a larger house with a smaller income, perhaps you can start a cooking school or rent out rooms for clubs charging extra for catering.

Living in Retirement

Hopefully by the time you retire you'll have enough of a nest egg to live comfortably in the way you want. You'll have the habit of reassessing your goals each year and making rational vision and virtue-based decisions to help you reach them.

The reason I mention this is that with a longer life as part of a global community, you have more options, and this means that retirement is not the time to throw caution to the wind and stop paying attention to your Wealth Management Cycle.

You still need to recast your vision and virtues, develop goals and Spending Plans to achieve them.

Stay at Home

One popular option is to stay in your family home. If you're planning to stay home, think about the accessibility renovations you might need like wheelchair access, accommodation for carers, lifts, or ground floor bathrooms.

Or as you get older, consider downsizing to a smaller, less expensive, more manageable home with these facilities plus access to assisted transportation and pharmacies that deliver.

Perhaps you'll be able to renovate your sprawling home into apartments you can rent out to older people like you, so you'll have your independence as well as some company.

And if you can generate enough interest, perhaps they'll pay to decorate the apartments to their own tastes. And maybe you will grow a waiting list too.

Find a New Home

Consider sharing a home with other people, moving into an apartment building, or an area well served with the kind of amenities you prefer within walking distance.

Enter an elder care community; not a nursing home, but a niche community. Like a retirement village, community of artists, or an intergenerational community similar to a village but with more shared facilities

Retire Offshore in Luxury

If you live in an affluent Western Country, you may find it significantly cheaper to retire abroad.

Of course, you have to carefully research your potential locations for the cost of living, particularly the cost and adequacy of medical care, and hiring home help.

Plus, visas, work, and residency requirements, language barriers, airports and transfers, climate, location, taxation, the size of the expatriate community, access to libraries, cultural and sporting events, transportation, cost and availability of restaurants.

You also need to consider whether you personally are flexible enough to adapt to a different way of life, or whether you are comfortable reinventing yourself.

Nursing Home/Residential Care Facility

At some point, you may need to enter a residential care facility, and as I write this, they're becoming less institutional.

However, nursing home care costs are escalating beyond the ability of many people to manage, particularly where you can't insure for it.

Even if you want to avoid a nursing home, you still need to think about how to pay for the care you will need.

Retirement Income

Retirement is also not the time to stop learning and investing your wealth. The last thing you want is to run out of money with twenty years to go.

Even if you're very careful, your circumstances will change over time.

Stay on top of government policy discussions, and consider the consequences for your retirement plans. Start reassessing your options when it looks like you'll be negatively impacted, but wait until the legislation passes before you act.

Learn as much as you can about minimising the tax payable on your investments (e.g., capital gains), and have your returns prepared by a professional who specialises in retirees.

Annuities

Annuities are a kind of investment product where you invest a lump sum to buy several years of regular payments. The investment may provide a fixed or variable return depending on whether the funds are invested in cash or stocks.

Their main benefits are the deferral of tax until the payments are made and a guaranteed income stream.

The drawbacks are that you cannot access your initial capital, have no control over how the funds are invested and will be paying a management or administration fee that is probably a percentage of your investment which will reduce your capital over time.

Pensions

Assuming State funded age pensions or retirement benefits still exist at that time. And are sufficient to at least cover your most basic costs.

Sharing

After retirement, you can share as much of your passive income that you don't need for your expenses (while preserving your capital investments). Or your assets, though try to keep enough to generate around 25 times your annual spend.

Summary

Your retirement could be a very long time. Maybe even longer than your working life. So start thinking and planning now:
- How are you going to fill your days? How well, and how rich do you need to be to pursue the activities you want to do.
- Where do you want to live? Can you afford it? Are you physically and mentally flexible enough to live there?
- What will you live off? What are the tax and income implications of those choices?

CHAPTER 20

Estate Planning

YOU MAY FIND THIS CHAPTER difficult because we're talking about making provisions for the disposal of your assets after you die.

I can tell you from my own experience that while it's hard coming to terms with your loss when a family member dies, it is almost impossible when you have to sort out their financial chaos as well.

Making a Will is one of the best risk management plans you can make, a final gift that gives you and your beneficiaries peace of mind, before and after your death.

However, estate planning should be more than just writing a Will. It should include consideration of tax implications and the assets that fall outside the scope of your Will (like joint, trust, and business).

And it should also make provision for the care of your young children and pets as well as consider the potential for future divorce and children from multiple marriages.

No one really likes thinking about their death, but it's your opportunity to give your family some breathing space – one last gift if you like.

Plus, it's your opportunity to plan the funeral you deserve!

Develop a Philosophy of Dying

This will probably just be an extension of the virtues you have been working within and, but it will guide your decisions.

You might continue to include the Environment with minimal preservation of your remains and a cardboard coffin.

Or add a commitment to speak honestly and openly about your death; giving your friends and family permission to exchange feelings and talk freely (for good or ill) about their unfinished business with you.

Preparing for the end of this life and the start of the next, within the context of your religious beliefs.

Start sharing your family history and stories; you might write this down, or make a recording.

Share the essence of yourself, your beliefs, and your virtues with your family if you're not already living them together.

Tell them what you hope for them - preferably in a way they'll want to hear; that they'll be happy, healthy and well-loved, rather than your specific hopes for a haircut, a nice wife and a flourishing dentistry practice.

You might like to plan your funeral, and include detailed instructions about what to do with your remains (cremation or burial), and how you would like your service conducted.

Your family will probably appreciate it if you designate a fund to pay for it, as even basic funerals can be expensive.

If you know where you want to be interred, buy the space now and make provisions for the memorial you want as well.

Living Will

A Living Will expresses your preferences for medical care should you be unable to speak for yourself; for example, do not resuscitate.

Depending on where you live, it might be called an Advanced Care Directive, a Medical Power of Attorney, or something similar.

It grants the person of your choice authority to make those decisions on your behalf. Choose someone you know will be strong enough to carry out your wishes when the time comes.

Most hospitals have an appropriate form for your jurisdiction. Once it's been completed, make sure that relevant family members and medical specialists get a copy as well.

Depending on your virtues, choose the treatment you prefer and make your wishes well known, for example, to have:
- Your life maintained regardless of the cost and possibility of recovery.
- Treatment administered until you have been in a persistent vegetative state for a period of time, and two doctors agree on your prognosis.
- Treatment withheld unless there is a better than 85% chance your full health is recoverable.

Discuss your end of life care with your family in the hope that they will endorse your do not resuscitate order and support your desire to donate your viable organs.

Or to die in your home with your pets and family nearby.

Intestacy

If you die without a legal Will, or your Will cannot be located, you are considered to have died intestate, and a Probate Court decides the division of your assets.

Most jurisdictions consider that you have died without a Will if you have not made a *formal* Will. However, you can write an informal Will which the Court will consider when determining what happens to your estate.

To give it the best possible chance, hand write it using one pen on a clean, unmarked piece of paper, with the date and your signature at the end. If you make a mistake, start again on a fresh sheet of paper.

As an executor has not been named, someone must apply for authorisation to administer the estate *before* any action can be taken to settle it.

Some jurisdictions require that they deposit a bond or obtain a guarantee before approval is granted.

While there are differences in the jurisdictions, Courts will generally split assets according to their ownership.

For example, if you and your current partner are living in a property you jointly own with your ex, the property will most likely be granted to your ex (depending on the purchase contract, see Chapter 15: Buying Property).

If you're the sole owner of your property, it may be split between your partner and the children of your previous relationship excluding the children of your current relationship.

Your joint bank account may transfer directly to your partner, or it may be held by the Court pending further investigation.

It will be difficult for everyone involved, so it's best to make arrangements before you die.

Wills

Your Will is basically a statement of what you want to happen to your stuff when you die.

However, as it has standing under the law, it involves dealings with Courts, and that means the results may not always be what you hope.

Depending on the complexity of your affairs, you can:
- Draw up a formal Will with an experienced Deceased Estate Lawyer.
- Buy a blank do-it-yourself Will kit.
- Use a computer program.

Regardless, it must be properly signed and witnessed; all of you in the same place at the time of the signing.

Depending on your jurisdiction, you will need two or three witnesses, but they can't be named as beneficiaries.

You can change your Will at any time with a Codicil describing the changes you want, similarly signed and witnessed.

The Codicil becomes part of the Will, so make sure that it is stored with the Will, but not stapled or taped to it.

You must name an executor, who is responsible for carrying out your Court approved wishes; selling your assets, paying your debts and distributing the balance to your beneficiaries.

It would be kind of you to check whether they're willing to take on this responsibility because it can be a challenging role.

On your death, most Wills undergo a Probate process where the Court confirms it conforms to the legal requirements.

If the Will is valid, the Court authorises the transfer of assets, so that once the formalities are complete, you are the legal owner of Aunty Eglantine's diamond bracelet or the title of Uncle Melvin's house can be transferred to you.

A simple estate might only take a couple of weeks to process, but a more complex one could take several years.

In the meantime, there are statutory fees (set by law) that need to be paid.

Some jurisdictions offer a cheaper and simpler process for small estates, so it's worth checking what the situation is where you live.

It's possible someone may contest your Will; they could challenge your guardianship arrangements, or feel entitled to a greater share of your assets than you've allocated them.

These issues are considered by the judge as part of the Probate process but could be referred to other Courts for resolution before coming back for authorisation.

Actions like these increase the length of time required and generally require a relevant legal professional(s) to act on your behalf. They will expect payment.

When you're writing your Will, be very specific about who gets which of your personal belongings. You could start including details of the beneficiaries in your annual inventory, or set up a dedicated inventory for just this goal.

Include your Will in your annual review to ensure it remains current; that you haven't sold your diamond bracelet in the meantime and that the right number of children are named.

Don't assume the right thing to do is to leave it all to your children.

Think about what you want for them right now; their jobs, their income, and consider what you would be willing to give them at school or college or as independent adults were you alive at the time.

Think about your sharing program and how you want to include those arrangements.

Discuss your plans with your family; encourage them to make suggestions but don't feel compelled to act on them unless you see some benefit in them.

And they're in keeping with your virtues and goals.

Don't let them make assumptions that will be dashed when your Will is read, and the estate wound up.

Trusts

One of the most effective ways to minimise tax and Probate issues is set up a trust fund and transfer your assets into it.

There are lots of different kinds of trusts around the world, so the following is just a general overview.

They're very complex legal and administrative tools, so if you want to set one up, I strongly encourage you to seek financial and legal advice from qualified local professionals.

The simplest explanation I've heard comes from Suze Orman. She says a trust is like a suitcase; you pack and unpack your assets during your life, each with a little label explaining who the asset belongs to. When you die, the new trustee opens the case for the beneficiaries to withdraw their assets.

Trusts are an excellent way to remove assets from your personal ownership. They don't belong to you anymore, so they're excluded from your tax considerations, the Probate process, and are protected from forced sale in payment of debts or legal action.

As the trust deed sets out how the assets will be disbursed, they can protect you and your beneficiaries from themselves.

While you're alive, you can act as the trustee, or nominate someone else to manage the fund (companies can charge by commission or fee, so choose wisely).

Additionally, all Court records, including Probated Wills become public records.

This is great news for genealogists and historians, but your beneficiaries may not care to share the knowledge that they are the recipient of your licentious jade collection.

Or have your video testimony explaining why you have excluded them going viral on YouTube.

What happens in the trust, stays in the trust.

Businesses

If you own or have interests in business, you need to think about how you are going to divest them. See Chapter 14: Owning a Business for more.

Children

Clearly, you need to think carefully about what happens to your children once you've gone.

Appoint guardians who will raise your children to be the caring, responsible adults with the virtues you hope for.

Try to ensure that the people spending money on their behalf are not the same people managing it (to avoid conflicts of interest).

Choose people your children can have respectful and cooperative relationships with.

If the inheritance will be large, consider a trust that will disburse the money in three instalments:
1. In the early twenties to fund lifestyle acquisitions like cars, vacations and shopping.
2. In the late twenties to fund asset accumulations like a home, or starting a business.
3. In the mid-thirties when it's more likely to go towards long-term goals or retirement planning.

Not that you can control how they spend it, but you can deliver it at different times of their lives where they're more likely to use it wisely than others.

Your Inheritances

Should you be fortunate enough to receive a legacy from someone else's estate, don't make any rash or hasty decisions that might lead you to fritter it away.

Give yourself a little to spend, but lock the rest away in a high-interest savings account you can't access for six to twelve months while you grieve and come to terms with your loss.

When the account matures, consider how you can best honour the memory of the person who left it to you. Would they want you to pay off your debts, get an education, or sail around the world for a year?

Given the choice, would they buy you a home, a significant piece of art, or invest it for your retirement?

You could also share some to a cause you both cared about.

Summary

Death comes to us all. Estate Planning allows you to take care of your friends and family once you've gone.
- Make peace with your death, and give your loved ones the opportunity to as well.
- Plan for your end of life medical care.
- Make a Will, and review it annually.
- Consider setting up a trust to manage your assets
- Think about how you can best care for your children.

Conclusion

WHEW! WE'VE COVERED A LOT.

But before you make any sudden sweeping changes to your financial life, there is some stuff you need to do.

- Give yourself some time to become aware of how and where you struggle with money; be gentle with yourself and don't nag.

    It took you this long to get messed up and it's going to take time for you and your unconscious to sort it out and prepare for the decisions you'll be making.

    When you two get your act together, you'll make appropriate decisions from a place of inner peace.

- Remember, the changes you make to your wealth management will have flow-on effects in other areas of your life.

    Your virtues-based focus will allow you to more easily express your truth and some people will find this hard to deal with.

They might not understand why you want to continue your education, live a healthier lifestyle, or change careers.

You'll need to give them some time to adjust, but it could be that you need to let them go along with your old habits.

- Acknowledge that you can't know everything and that sometimes the best option is to pay for expert opinion.

  It would be insane for me to rely on the internet for information about how to manage my kidney transplant, so I employ a variety of professionals who have devoted their lives to developing the knowledge and skills that I need.

  In just the same way as you use a car mechanic, there are times when you need legal and financial professionals to fill those gaps.

By reading this book, you've taken the first step towards a happier and more fulfilling future.

Establishing your wealth management cycle, puts you on the path to achieving your bright shiny vision.

You know where you're going, and how to get there.

And I hope that it turns out to be everything you wish for.

Appendix A: Miss Baker

Emily Baker is a single woman in her mid-twenties. She lives at home with her parents but pays them board. She continues to perform her childhood chores, does her own laundry, and eats the meals her mother prepares. She has a college degree and an entry-level job in a big company.

Vision Statement

Emily hopes to meet a nice boy and get married, but first, she wants to get her own place. Not necessarily buy right now because she wants to pay off her student debt and travel as well, but a little place that she doesn't have to share, and can come and go as she pleases.

Her vision statement could be

> "I live debt-free in an inexpensive, cosy apartment with red geraniums on my window sill. My lovely neighbours water my plants when I travel."

Mission Statement

> "Commit to an abundant future with a Spending Plan that pays off debt quickly and maximises long-term savings."

Virtues Statement

While Emily wants marriage and a family someday, the virtues her statements suggest are important to her in the short-term are Independence, Prosperity and Freedom.

If she was inclined, she might add Affection and Friendship, or just leave it at three virtues for the moment.

She could also go a little further and define what they look like for the next couple of years, for example, Independence could mean developing self-reliance, or Prosperity learning about wealth management.

Wealth Management Goals

With her vision of independence, and mission of an Abundant future, Emily has done some research and discovered that apartment rentals range from $500 - $1,000 per month, with establishment costs about the same.

Before she signs a lease, she wants to practice paying rent so she (and her parents) can be assured it's affordable, so she'll be attempting to save the equivalent of rent each month. But she wants to move somewhere nice (and safe), and will stretch her monthly savings goal to $1,100.

At the end of the year, she'll have achieved the habit of living on less and saved her deposit and first month's rent. She'll also have $13,200 she can use for establishment costs, to buy homewares for her new home, take a trip, or pay down her student loans.

Her SMART goal becomes:

> "This year, I will bank $1,100 each month in a high-interest savings account."

Wealth Goal Planning

Emily's goal is relatively straightforward; she can open a dedicated savings account and have part of her pay deposited into it. She could even make it an account that's harder to withdraw from, for example, one that doesn't have an ATM card, or where she has to wait 24 hours for the funds to be transferred to her everyday account.

Clothing Department Spending

Lucky Emily gets this all to herself! But as this is her first job, she'll need to think carefully about how she spends it.

Controlling Spending

Emily's priority is saving her apartment rental each month. Any slippage implies an inability to pay her rent, so this is a significant concern. If her savings are slipping, she needs to choose between a reduction in the quality of apartment she can afford or adjusting her spending so that she can save more.

She might notice that she has been going out with her friends a lot and choose to socialise less, or suggest that sometimes they stay home for pizza. Or if she notices that she has made a lot of impulse clothing purchases while buying lunch, she might bring lunch from home and avoid the shops.

Emily enjoys making jewellery; chandelier earrings are her speciality. She has made a lot and could consider selling them as a side business to bring in a little extra income. She is making them anyway, but there will be a cost in time and money to set up a market stall or list them on a craft site like Etsy.

Petty Cash/Pocket Money

Emily may not need more than $100 for her morning coffees, the odd lunch and an after-work drink.

Cost/Benefit Spending

Emily picks up a couple of things at the supermarket on her way home because it's quick and easy.

Saving Money

If Emily does not nurture her vision of living in her own apartment, it will never happen.

Emergency Credit Card Limit

Emily is young and single. Even when she moves into a place of her own, she is unlikely to need more than around $1,000 to cover a car or appliance breakdown.

Appendix B: The Smiths

Bob and Amanda Smith are married, have two children (Daniel 8, Lisa 6), and a dog named Toby. They live in a mortgaged house in the suburbs. Bob commutes to the city, and Amanda takes care of the house and children. Now that both children are at school, she volunteers at their school.

Vision Statement

Bob and Amanda are concerned about the world their children are growing up in. The air and water are polluted, the climate is changing, and there are additives in the food. They worry about the quality of education and feel they are not living in the kind of village that they want bringing up their children.

They feel a move to a more rural location might be best, somewhere with a large yard to play in, plenty of space to grow fruit, vegetables and chickens. Somewhere in a close-knit community with a good school.

The Smith vision could be

> "We are part of a close-knit rural community, growing healthy produce, and the children are receiving a good independent education."

Mission Statement

> "Prioritise the children's long-term interests with a healthier and happier lifestyle in a cleaner nutritive environment."

Virtues Statement

Clearly, Bob and Amanda think Family is the most important, and following (or because of) this, Health, Education, and Community or perhaps Connection.

Wealth Management Goals

With the vision of moving to a cleaner, close-knit community and the mission of prioritising the children's interests, the Smiths decide it's time to move.

While they want to do it immediately, they agree it will be for the long-term, so they must be sure it's the right place.

They decide to research what they need, and where their needs can be met.

Their HARD goal is:

> "We will shortlist five potential communities by the end of the year."

Wealth Goal Planning

The Smiths have accidentally set themselves an enormous goal. The best way to proceed is to break the bigger goal into smaller steps within a logical framework. They should agree some responsibilities and time frames and put them in their calendars to make sure that they progress their goal.

For example, start by deciding some respectful communication ground rules. Allowing a month to agree their "must have" and "nice to have" attributes, and another to identify preferred and no-go countries or states. After a year of investigating the relative merits and cost of living in each area, they can rank them and pick their preferred location.

Clothing Department Spending

The Smith family would proportionally split it between them (say Bob 35%, Amanda 23%, Daniel 22%, and Lisa 20%).

Controlling Spending

The Smiths are focused on relocating. Their research program might involve additional costs that they haven't planned for, like phone calls and internet access, magazines and other research materials, plus trips to scout out potential locations. They may be noting these as incidentals and when they realise how much it's costing choose to recast their Spending Plan to make a particular department for it.

Some of these additional costs have come from existing provisions for operating costs, but things like the travel would be from savings. As the move will be in the new year and may involve a different climate they might cut back their clothing spend rather than buy clothes (or shoes) that may not work in their new location. They could also start pulling back on some of the local groups and activities they are involved with.

While Amanda does make a lovely cake, the costs (in time and money) of making them on a commercial basis are unfeasible. However, as they are planning to move, they can start decluttering and selling off some of the possessions they don't believe need to come with them.

Petty Cash/Pocket Money

Amanda might need $300 for child and household incidentals, as well as pocket money for the kids.

Cost/Benefit Spending

The Smiths might choose to take the children to the farm to see how food is grown.

Saving Money

If Bob and Amanda do not cultivate their vision of a rural retreat, they will be stuck in suburbia for years to come.

Emergency Credit Card Limit

The Smiths might need as much as $10,000 in case Amanda has to stay in a hotel in the City while Daniel or Lisa is in hospital.

Risk Management Plan (tree falls on house)

- **Likelihood:** If the Smith's new property is partly forested, a tree might fall on the house during a storm. It would have to be a big storm, so the likelihood is Possible.
- **Severity:** The Smiths are likely to have only a portion of the building damaged. Depending on the season they could make the house safe themselves while they wait for a builder to make proper repairs. Their scenario is Fair.
- **Risk Prioritisation:** Possible by Fair which is High risk.
- **Recovery Plan:** The Smiths could pre-screen builders, stockpile tarpaulins and other quick fix materials, and ensure Toby is unable to escape the property.

Appendix C: The Butchers

Ash and Jo are an older couple who've been in a committed relationship for 25 years. They live together in an inner-city apartment with their cats Tiger and Shadow. They both work long hours in upper-management jobs, so they eat out most of the time.

Vision Statement

As they approach their retirement, Ash and Jo don't feel that they spend enough time together. They want to nurture their relationship and pursue an activity together, perhaps cooking, or taking a Spanish class so they can travel. Maybe walk the 500-mile (790 km) Camino de Santiago, though they acknowledge they would need to build their fitness and stamina for that. They would like to have a more active role in the lives of their nieces and nephews.

Their vision statement might be

> "A long, happy and healthy life, enjoying indoor and outdoor activities together. Building an enormous memory bank to share with our family."

Mission Statement

> "Treasuring our relationship by enjoying time together; getting fit, hiking in the country, cooking and speaking Spanish."

Virtues Statement

Ash and Jo have recognised they're in danger of losing touch with each other, and want to make their relationship their top priority so their first Virtue may be Love, Relationship, or Romance. And as they want to work on it together, an-other could be Teamwork.

They're focusing on cooking and an activity that requires a high level of fitness so they could round it out with Health or Well-being.

Wealth Management Goals

Ash and Jo want to focus on the Virtues of Love, Teamwork and Health by cooking a meal together at home once a week.

Their GET BETTER goal becomes:

> "We will grow our relationship by preparing and eating healthy food together."

Wealth Goal Planning

Ash and Jo's goal is both easy and hard at the same time. They need to find some local classes at times they can both make, and schedule these along with Date Night as priority weekly appointments. They will need a conscious, ongoing focus (e.g., packing up and leaving work "early") until it becomes an automatic response.

Clothing Department Spending

Ash and Jo would work out some sort of split, perhaps according to job seniority.

Controlling Spending

The Butchers are starting to think about a potential future where they aren't working. They're planning activities to reconnect with each other, and improve their health. They can enjoy these now, as well as expand them to fill uncommitted time in the future.

These are also relatively inexpensive activities in comparison to frequently going out for drinks and meals with friends and colleagues. They might find that they are spending less than expected and can divert these funds towards their retirement or travel savings. This is a useful thing to note, as it indicates that they may find it easier to transition to a more limited retirement income.

At this point, they don't need additional income, but it might be useful for them to consider what they could do to supplement their retirement. This might be looking for a business they could run, or starting to invest in products that will provide income.

Petty Cash/Pocket Money

Ash and Jo could have been carrying $500 each, but drop it down to $250 to bring their focus back home to each other.

Cost/Benefit Spending

The Butchers might use a subscription service because they live in the inner city and don't have a car.

Saving Money

If Ash and Jo don't nurture their dream of travelling the world together, they will be working until they drop dead.

Emergency Credit Card Limit

Jo might need to fly cross-country to spend time with a dying parent. And as Ash travels for work, they might be better with separate $15,000 credit cards while they wait for the expense claims to be paid out.

Risk Management Plan (tree falls on house)

- **Likelihood:** The Butcher's inner-city apartment would need some kind of fantastical event to cause a tree to fall on their home, so the likelihood is Rare.
- **Severity:** If the Butcher's building is damaged by a falling tree, they could be denied access for months, and potentially forced to pay their mortgage and rent somewhere to live at the same time which would be Tragic!
- **Risk Prioritisation:** Rare by Tragic is High risk.
- **Recovery Plan:** The Butcher's might move in with Ash's sister for a couple of weeks until they know what's happening, save a few thousand dollars (so they have money available for an immediate move), and stay in contact with their real estate agent friend. They may have to put Tiger and Shadow in their usual cattery.

Appendix D: Sample House Deposit Spending Plan

Many countries share the dream of property ownership.

Most often it rises from returning servicemen wanting to live the good life they fought to defend.

It was partly to create a comfy family nest, partly to prevent the land going to "undesirables", and partly an asset to draw on in hard times.

And for this, you'd save a house deposit, and take out a mortgage for the rest.

Vision, Mission, Virtues

Circumstances are different now, but most people still hope to buy a home of some description of their own.

Vision

There are a lot of reasons you might want to buy property, and as everything else feels so insecure, we're going to see

> A secure future in a home of our own. (Where the sun always shines on the green grass and we're always happy.)

Mission

In the meantime, we'll create a regular savings and investment plan.

Virtues

Saving is always harder than spending, so Focus, Reliability, and Discipline.

Goal

There are two ways to save your house deposit:
- Save what you think you can afford.
- Work out how much you need, then using a SMART goal (e.g., $X per pay for Y years) to get there.

If you really want to buy property (as opposed to take a trip for example), I recommend the SMART goal.

Basic Spending Plan

Assuming an after-tax monthly income of $3,435, your basic plan might look like this:

Department	% of Income	Amount
Food	25%	$859
Housing	20%	$687
Clothing	15%	$515
Operations	15%	$515
Happiness	25%	$859
TOTAL	100%	$3,435

Considerations

The common wisdom is to start by working out how much you can borrow.

It's a reasonable enough place to start, but at that point, most people tend to decide that's how much they're going to spend and shop accordingly.

But your home is probably the most significant purchase you'll make, and you're committing decades to paying it off.

Why not decide what kind of house you'd like, find out what it might cost and then decide whether you can afford it.

Compare smaller properties, that need renovation or are in less expensive areas.

Consider whether it's worth paying more to live closer to public transport, or less to live in a new subdivision with fewer facilities.

How Much Do You Need to Save?

For the sake of convenience, in Australia, my sample wage could be eligible for a $405,000 loan.

Depending on how fussy you are, you could buy a three-bedroom, one-bathroom house from $300,000.

Let's say you're looking for a $400,000 home.

You'll need a minimum deposit of 5% ($20,000) and your repayments over 30 years, @ 5% will be $1,020/month.

A deposit this small may cost you a higher interest rate, will cost mortgage insurance and could reduce your chances of getting a mortgage.

The total cost of your deposit, fees and charges is $59,200.

Your chances of getting a mortgage are better with a bigger deposit.

At 20% ($80,000) your repayments over 30 years, @ 5% will be $859/month. Plus you won't pay mortgage insurance.

Total cost (including deposit) $105,216.

Let's aim high and say $105,000 as a house deposit.

Which leaves us with a range of possible savings targets:

$$$	Months	
$8,750	12	Let's work with $1,094/month over eight years. Though if you've been renting, your lender will take that commitment into account.
$1,750	60 (5 years)	
$1,094	96 (8 years)	
$875	120 (10 years)	

How Much Can You Save?

Another thing that people tend to do when saving for a house deposit, is ruthlessly cut expenses.

Which again is fine, but:
- You eliminate your capacity to deal with the unexpected,
- You live a poor and miserable existence while you're saving, and
- Borrow money based on the financial assumption you'll be living the same poor and miserable existence for the term of the loan.

It's understandable because modern spending is often subscriptions direct debited to your accounts, and you'll probably face some moral questioning about whether your $15/month streaming subscription is necessary.

But;
- It's cheaper than going to the pictures, and
- You'll appreciate it when your mortgage repayments are so large you can't afford to go to the pictures.

Work Out How Much You Can Pay

Take a look at your expenses, and weigh them up against your Vision, virtues and goals. Where can you sustainably reduce your costs over the long-term?

- **Food:** If you've been living a normal life, you've probably been eating take out. You could be radical and cut this by $200/month, but let's cut the snack food, allow the odd night off and cut by $199/month.

- **Housing:** With an eight-year time-frame it might be worth relocating to cut costs – how about testing a suburb with purchase potential?
- **Clothing:** In all likelihood, you have more clothes than you wear. Try to mix it up a bit and cut $215/month.
- **Operations:** Look at cuts to things like your phone plan or changing utility providers. Let's try for another $130.
- **Happy Life:** This is technically already savings – it pays for your streaming service, the gym, and so on. As I mentioned, we're still talking sustainable, so it's going to be things like vacations, education and gifts. Let's take $550.

Which gives you $1,094 a month over eight years.

Work Out How to Save

When you have a savings target like this, that's going to take several years to achieve, think about how you can make your savings work harder, potentially reducing the amount of time you have to save for.

And when it comes to getting a mortgage, your lender looks at the frequency as well as the amount of your savings, so start with a scheduled deposit; ideally wages, into a designated savings account with a high interest rate.

And after a few months, when you've got a few thousand, start looking for higher interest rates.

Potential House Deposit Holistic Spending Plan

There's quite a significant change in expenditure which is bound to be quite shocking initially and may need some working up to.

Department	% of Income	Amount
Food	19%	$660
Housing	20%	$687
Clothing	9%	$300
Operations	11%	$385
Happiness	41%	$1,403
TOTAL	**100%**	**$3,435**

Outcome

This is one possible way to save a house deposit.

You will, of course, adjust the figures according to what else is going on in your life.

And how much support you are offered and willing to take from those around you.

There are more sample spending plans at https://www.alexandriablaelock.com/books/holistic-personal-finance/.

Glossary

Asset: something that has a financial value which is managed for a future benefit like generating income or reducing spending. In personal terms, they can be:
- Current (easily converted to cash in the short-term, e.g., savings accounts, stocks or other investment vehicles like bonds, art, jewellery or antiques).
- Fixed (long-term investments like your house or other real estate).

Balance Sheet: see Statement of Net Worth.

Bond: basically, an IOU: you lend money to a borrower who agrees to pay you periodic interest, and return your capital on a given date in the future.

Brawn: your physical strength; ability to lift and carry things.

Budget: an estimate of costed expenditure. See also Spending Plan.

Capital: the cash and assets you have available for generating wealth (that exceeds your needs). See also Return.

Compounding Interest: interest is calculated on the principal (or debt) plus the accumulated interest.

Contingency Plan: a plan of action to take when a risk becomes imminent. See also Risk Management Plan.

Cost of Living: a calculation each jurisdiction makes about how much it costs to maintain a given standard of living.

Cost per Use: a way of calculating the value of an item by dividing the cost price by the number of times it is used. For example, if you purchase an item for $100 and use it once, the cost per use is $100. If you use it 50 times, the cost per use is $2. The item you use 50 times provides better value because you get more use before it is used up. See also Price and Value.

Credit: in accounting terms, this is an amount that you owe for goods you have taken without payment.

Creditor: the person or business you owe credit (money) to.

Debt Reduction Plan: a plan for systematically reducing and eliminating your debts.

Debtor: the person or business that owes you money.

Deficit: at the end of the year, more money was spent than came in. You owe money.

Disaster Recovery Plan: see Recovery Plan.

Dollar Cost Averaging: investing the same amount of money in a particular investment at regular intervals. You buy more when the price is low and less when it is high, but when sold, all achieve the same price.

Emergency Plan: a plan for responding to an emergency situation. For example, the circumstances that you will remain to defend your property (e.g., bushfire but not flood), the tools you will need, and the steps you will take.

Expenditure: the act of making a payment (or payments). Also as a past tense of expense; items that have been paid for.

End: the result you want, for example, to be in Spain. See also Means.

Estate Plan: a plan for managing your affairs after your die. It includes your Will, arrangements for your children, pets, business and so on.

Expense: the cost for something you have bought, a service you have received, or a fee or charge you have incurred.

Financial Freedom: you are managing your assets and liabilities, and have a savings cushion. You have a comfortable life but are dependent on paid work.

Financial Independence: the state following Financial Freedom; you are not dependent on paid work for income. You might choose to work, but are managing your assets to produce sufficient income to meet your needs. There are no significant financial impediments to your choices.

Fixed Costs: costs like your rent, loans, or insurances that do not change a great deal over time. See also Variable Costs.

Flourishing: an awareness of growing and developing, reaching to become more than you were before.

Health Care Plan: a plan for managing a period of treatment for a serious condition such as cancer. It includes personal and medical care and treatments.

Investment Plan: your strategy for growing your investment portfolio according to your investment philosophy, asset allocation and quality standards. See also Savings Plan.

Jurisdiction: the territory in which laws are enforced, for example, your country or state.

Law of Diminishing Returns: an economic term describing the decrease in the incremental output of a production process in relation to the incremental increase in a single factor of production. If all else remains the same, increasing one component will eventually reduce production per unit of component; each unit of output costs more because the input is used less efficiently. For example, too many cooks spoil the broth.

Liability: a responsibility to pay on demand or at a certain date or event. It can be:
- Short-term: payable within 12 months
- Long-term: due after a year

The most common kinds are credit/store cards, loans and leases.

Means: any method for getting what you want (your end), for example, taking an aeroplane to get to Spain. See also End.

Monte Carlo Simulation: a technique for understanding risk and uncertainty. As a method for forecasting, it introduces an element of random unpredictability into the results. It uses three prediction scenarios (best case, worst-case, and most likely based on historic data) to produce a range of possible outcomes. These are fed into the simulation to return the likelihood as a percentage, for example, a 64% likelihood that an investment return will be greater than 5%.

Philanthropy: a concern for human welfare, usually demonstrated by charitable or benevolent donations to organisations that work with less fortunate people. May also include endowments to hospitals, arts institutions, or universities. See also Sharing.

Price: the cost of goods and services, generally considered objective, but fluctuates over the short-term according to availability. See also Cost per Use and Value.

Profit: the money left over when you've paid your expenses.

Purchasing Plan: a strategic approach to buying necessary goods and services that ensures purchases are made at the right time and in the right places.

Recovery Plan: a description of the steps, costs and time required to get back to normal after a setback.

Retirement Plan: a strategic plan to save and invest the money to fund your Financial Independence lifestyle. It may also include details about managing your health, and developing the skills and experience you will need to pursue activities after retirement.

Return: a repayment of capital from an investment. It is generally an amount that exceeds the growth of the investment and is called a "capital gain" rather than income and taxed on that basis. See also Capital.

Risk Management Plan: a plan identifying the major risks, assessing their likelihood, and severity as well as strategies to treat them. The plan offers the opportunity to reduce risks, and consequences as well as deal with the situation at the time and recover after. See also Contingency Plan.

Savings Plan: a strategic approach to saving towards goals. It includes targets, instalments, and account types. See also Investment Plan.

Shares: see Stock.

Sharing: intentionally giving your time, labour, or money for the benefit of others. See also Philanthropy.

Spending Plan: a spending forecast that helps you decide whether you can afford unplanned spending. See also Budget.

Statement of Net Worth: a summary of your assets minus your liabilities at a given moment in time.

Statutory: prescribed by law.

Stock: a share of a company, which entitles you to a share of the company profits.

Surplus: at the end of the year, more money came in than was spent. You have money left over.

Value: a subjective and rarely changing interpretation of material worth based on long-term practical usefulness. Alternatively, how much money goods can be converted into. See also Cost per Use and Price.

Variable Costs: costs like electricity, cell phones, and food that can vary a great deal from bill to bill according to how much you use them. See also Fixed Costs.

Virtue: a centre of excellence, an important skill or attitude that takes a lot of time and effort to get good at.

Wealth: abundance of anything (e.g., a wealth of experience). In the Middle Ages, wealth meant happiness (from the root word weal, meaning well-being).

Will: a document that describes how your property is to be divided when you die.

Bibliography

Association for Psychological Science. "Take notes by hand for better long-term comprehension." ScienceDaily. www.sciencedaily.com/releases/2014/04/140424102837.htm (accessed March 28, 2017).

Beecher, Catherine E. 1848. *A Treatise on Domestic Economy, for the Use of Young Women at Home, and at School.* Revised ed. New York: Harper & Brothers Publishers.

Blaelock, Alexandria. 2015. *Build Your Signature Wardrobe: How to look good and feel confident in four steps.* Melbourne: BlueMere Books.

Brown, Clair. 1994. *American Standards of Living 1918 - 1988.* Oxford: Blackwell.

Bruère, Martha Bensley, and Robert W. Bruère. 1912. *Increasing Home Efficiency.* New York: The MacMillan Company.

Capgemini. 2017. *World Wealth Report 2017.* https://www.worldwealthreport.com (accessed October 26, 2017).

Drake, Susan M. and Monica Davidson. 2008. *Freelancing for Australians for Dummies.* Milton: Wiley Publishing Australia Pty Ltd.

Frederick, Christine. 1923. *Household Engineering: Scientific Management in the Home.* Chicago: American School of Home Economics.

Haskins, C.W. 1903. *How to Keep Household Accounts: A Manual of Family Finance.* New York: Harper & Brothers Publishers.

Hillis, Marjorie. 1937. *Orchids on Your Budget: or Live Smartly on What Have You*. Indianapolis: The Bobbs-Merrill Company.

Kessel, Brent. 2008. *It's Not About The Money: Unlock Your Money Type to Achieve Spiritual and Financial Abundance*. New York: HarperCollins.

Lawson, Dorie McCullough. 2004. "Who Wants to Be a Billionaire? A Rockefeller's rules for raising responsible children." Smithsonian Magazine. https://www.smithsonianmag.com/history/who-wants-to-be-a-billionaire-2996641 (accessed March 5, 2017).

Lino, Mark, Kevin Kuczynski, Nestor Rodriguez, and TusaRebecca Schap. 2017. *Expenditures on Children by Families, 2015*. Miscellaneous Publication No. 1528-2015. U.S. Department of Agriculture, Center for Nutrition Policy and Promotion. https://www.cnpp.usda.gov/sites/default/files/expenditures_on_children_by_families/crc2015.pdf (accessed 14 June, 2019).

Michalowicz. Mike. 2013. *The Toilet Paper Entrepreneur: The tell-it-like-it-is guide to cleaning up in business, even if you are at the end of your roll*. Boonton: Obsidian Launch LLC.

Maslow, Abraham. 1954. *Motivation and Personality*. New York, NY: Harper.

Orman, Suze. 2000. *The 9 Steps to Financial Freedom: Practical & Spiritual Steps So You Can Stop Worrying*. New York: Three Rivers Press.

Pape, Scott. 2007. *The Barefoot Investor: Five Steps to Financial Freedom*. 2nd ed. North Melbourne: Pluto Press Australia.

Pepper, Carol, and Camilla Webster. 2012. *The Seven Pearls of Financial Wisdom: A Woman's Guide to Enjoying Wealth and Power*. New York: St Martin's Press.

Pratchett, Terry. 2001. *The Thief of Time*. London: Doubleday.

Richards, Ellen H. 1915. *The Cost of Living as Modified by Sanitary Science*. 3rd ed. New York: John Wiley & Sons Inc.

Robin, Vicki and Joe Dominguez. 2008. *Your Money or Your Life: 9 Steps to Transforming Your Relationship with Money and Achieving Financial Independence*. Rev. ed. Revised and updated by Vicki Robin and Monique Tilford. New York: Penguin Books.

St John, Noah. 2014. *Afformations®: The Miracle of Positive Self-Talk*. 4th ed. Carlsbad: Hay House Inc.

The National Council for Research on Women. 2009. *Women in Fund Management: A Road Map for Achieving Critical Mass – and Why it Matters*. New York. http://txwsw.com/docs/women_fund_mgt.pdf (accessed October 26, 2017).

The University of Stavanger. "Better learning through handwriting." *ScienceDaily*. www.sciencedaily.com/releases/2011/01/110119095458.htm (accessed March 28, 2017).

United Nations, Department of Economic and Social Affairs, Population Division. (2015). *World Population Prospects: The 2015 Revision*, Volume I: Comprehensive Tables (ST/ESA/SER.A/379). https://esa.un.org/unpd/wpp/Publications/Files/WPP2015_Volume-I_Comprehensive-Tables.pdf

Index

Balance Sheet ...*See* Statement of Net Worth
Bank Reconciliation .... *See* Reconciliation
Books
   bank reconciliation 56
   cash reconciliation 56
   daily spend 51
   keeping 49
   reconciling 56
   simple 50
   spending plan reconciliation 57
   two page combined journal ledger 54
   two page department journal ledger 52
Borrowing
   counselling 138
   debt reduction plan ... 132–36
   debt types 130
   emergency credit card 132
      Baker 133
      Butcher 133
      Smith 133
   to pay off debt 136
      mortgage 137
      retirement fund 137
Business
   calculating income 178
   financing 179
   hybrid 175
   making a profit 179
   minimising costs 179
   offline 175
   online 175
   product based 174
   running 177
   service based 174
   transition from employment 176
   transitioning out 181

working in v working on 177
Buying .... *See* Purchasing
Can You Afford Your Life? 36
Cash Reconciliation .... *See* Reconciliation
Changing Your Behaviour 124
Children
   acting careers 219
   modelling careers 219
   sporting careers 219
   teaching about money 213–16
   Wills 248
Compound Interest 97
Conscious 120
Contingencies 59
Costs 37–39
   children 210
   dating 194
   fixed 37
   living 211
   necessary 38
   parenthood 208
   pregnancy 211
   schooling 212
   university 212
   unnecessary 38
   variable 37
   wedding 203
Dating 194
   Charming 196
   Humperdinck 195
   might last 198
   prenuptial 201
Departments
   choosing 32
   clothing 33, 40
   food 33, 40
   happy life 33, 41
   housing 33, 40
   incidentals 34
   operating costs 33, 41

Disaster Recovery Plan .. 160–61
Divorce
  initiating 225
  post 226
  pre 224
Dollar Cost Averaging 104
Dying
  intestacy 244
  living Will 243
  philosophy 242
  Will 245
Eating 165
Exercising 166
Fear 126
Fixed Costs .... See Costs
Furry Kids 220
Goal Frameworks 20
  better 22
  Buffet strategy 24
  HARD 21
  long term 22
  SMART 20
  stretch 23
Goal Planning 26
  Baker 26
  Butcher 27
  Smith 26
Goal Reviews 27
Health
  eating 165
  exercising 166
  manage risk 164
  meditation 167
  personal development .169
  relaxation 167
  sleeping 166
  stress 170
House Deposit
  sample spending plan .. 265
How Your Mind Works ... 120
Incidentals 34
Income
  minimum viable 43
  unreliable 42
Inner Child 122
Intestacy 244
Investing

choosing advisers 108
developing a plan ... 99–110
dollar cost averaging ... 104
future proofing 109
getting out 108
not getting out 106
policy 101–4
Labour Exchange 2
Lifespan
  average 152
Living Will 243
Meditation 167
Memories 121
Minimum Viable Income 43
Mission Statement 15
  Baker 15
  Butcher 16
  Smith 15
Necessary Costs .... See Costs
Needs and Wants 38
Parenthood
  blended families 216–18
  children
    acting careers 219
    modelling careers ... 219
    sporting careers 219
  costs 208
    children 210
    living 211
    schooling 212
    university 212
  pets 220
  pregnancy 211
  stay at home 209
  teaching about money
    213–16
  working 209
Pay Yourself First 97
Personal Development 169
Personal Risks
  death 149
  illness 147
  residential care 151
Pets 220
Philosophy
  dying 242
  investment 101
  means/ends 4

of life 169
Pocket Money 80
   Baker 81
   Butcher 81
   Smith 81
Prenuptial Agreement 201
Probate 246
   trusts 247–48
Property
   buying 188
   commerical 187
   mortgages 191
   ownership
      community 188
      joint tenancy 187
      sole 187
      tenants in common. 188
   residential 187
   sample house deposit
      spending plan 265
   saving a deposit 190
   vacant land 186
Purchasing
   agent 82
   bulk 89
   learning 85
   plan 81
      developing 83–85
   virtues 87
   what 87
   where 89
Reconciliation
   bank/cash 56
   spending plan 57
Records
   family
      medical 74
      personal 73
   household
      decorations 73
      financial 71
      hints 73
      important documents 71
      inventory 72
      library 73
      purchasing 73
      storage 73
   other

      addresses 74
      cooking 75
      crafting 75
      first aid 74
Reframe Your Thinking ... 127
Relaxation 167
Retirement
   income 239
      annuities 239
      pensions 239
   living 237
      home 237
      new home 237
      offshore 238
      residential care 238
   planning 231–36
   savings 233
   sharing 240
Review
   credit reference files 67
   estate planning 68
   financial 64
   general 67
   goals 67
   inventory 67
   investments 68
   risk management 68
   vision/mission/virtues.. 67
   will 68
Risk
   contingency plan 146
   events 142
   likelihood 142
   managing 144
   prioritisation 144
   recovery plan 146
   severity 142
Risk Management
   disaster recovery plan
      160–61
   in business 140
   planning 141–46
   your role 141
Risks
   health 164
   household
      damage 153
      injury 155

theft 154
identity theft 156
kidnapping 158
personal
  death 149
  injury 147
  residential care 151
Sample House Deposit
Spending Plan 265
Savings
  accounts 96
  compound interest 97
  pay yourself first 97
  planning 95–99
  property deposit 190
  retirement 233
  sample house deposit
    spending plan 265
  strategy 98
Sharing
  how 114
  how much 115
  retirement 240
  what 113
  when 114
  who with 115
  why 113
Sleeping 166
Spending
  controlling 58
    Baker 60
    Butcher 61
    Smith 60
  monitoring 57
  plan
    developing 32–42
    reconciliation 57
    tailoring 39
    unreliable income 42
    what is a 30

why needed 31
purchasing agent 82
what business does 81
Statement of Net Worth 64
Stress 170
Subconscious 120
Teaching Your Children
  About Money 213–16
Transactions 48
Trusts 247–48
  Probate 247–48
Unconscious 120
  examining 122
  memories 121
Unnecessary Costs ..See Costs
Unreliable Income 42
Variable Costs .... See Costs
Virtues Statement 16
  Baker 17
  Butcher 18
  Smith 17
Vision Statement 12
  Baker 13
  Butcher 14
  Smith 13
Wealth Management
  as a couple 203
  goals 23, 258
    Baker 25
    Butcher 26
    Smith 25
Wedding 203
When Things Are Dire 43
Will 245
  children 248
  intestacy 244
  living 243
  your inheritance 249
Your Future Self 232

Author's Note

Thanks again for buying my book.

If you'd like to let me know what you think, drop me a line at hello@alexandriablaelock.com.

I find people who offer irrelevant generic advice irritating. Particularly advice like saving money by brown bagging lunch or skipping takeout coffee. Especially given I work from home!

I believe the only person who can decide whether sacrificing take out coffee is the right choice for you, is you. If take out coffee makes you happy, why not cut back on something else instead?

You'll find some examples of how you might do this at alexandriablaelock.com/books/holistic-personal-finance/.

I've also set up a Pinterest board for other interesting information I find about paying for the life you want at www.pinterest.com.au/alexblaelock/holistic-personal-finance/.

For more, visit me at alexandriablaelock.com to:

- read my blog

- sign up for *Letters from my Library* to stay up to date on the development and release of my books. You'll also get research interestingness (that doesn't get to the blog), gossip about my writing life, and the odd special offer.

About the Author

Alexandria Blaelock writes self-help books applying business techniques to personal matters like getting dressed, cleaning house, and feeding your friends.

She also writes short stories, some of them for *Ellery Queen's Mystery Magazine* and *Pulphouse Fiction Magazine*.

As a recovering Project Manager, she's probably too fond of sticking to plan. She lives in a forest because she enjoys birdsong, the scent of gum leaves and the sun on her face.

When not telecommuting to parallel universes from her Melbourne based imagination, she watches K-dramas, talks to animals, and drinks Campari. At the same time.

Discover more at www.alexandriablaelock.com.

www.ingramcontent.com/pod-product-compliance
Lightning Source LLC
Chambersburg PA
CBHW071600080526
44588CB00010B/968